William Reed, Alfred Garnett Mortimer

Catholic Dogma

The Fundamental Truths of Revealed Religion

William Reed, Alfred Garnett Mortimer

Catholic Dogma
The Fundamental Truths of Revealed Religion

ISBN/EAN: 9783743410176

Manufactured in Europe, USA, Canada, Australia, Japa

Cover: Foto ©Lupo / pixelio.de

Manufactured and distributed by brebook publishing software (www.brebook.com)

William Reed, Alfred Garnett Mortimer

Catholic Dogma

CATHOLIC DOGMA

THE FUNDAMENTAL TRUTHS

OF

REVEALED RELIGION

Lectures

DELIVERED IN 1891 UNDER THE AUSPICES OF THE CHURCH
CLUB OF NEW YORK

NEW YORK
E. & J. B. YOUNG & CO.
COOPER UNION, FOURTH AVENUE
1892

COPYRIGHTED, 1892,
By E. & J B. YOUNG & CO.

CONTENTS.

LECTURE I.

THE NATURE OF DOGMA AND ITS OBLIGATION, .   3
*The Right Rev. A. N. Littlejohn, D.D., LL.D.,
Bishop of Long Island.*

LECTURE II.

THE HOLY TRINITY, ... 37
*The Rev. W. R. Huntington, D.D., Rector of Grace
Church, New York.*

LECTURE III.

THE INCARNATION, ... 67
*The Rev. Alfred G. Mortimer, D.D., Rector of St.
Mark's Church, Philadelphia.*

LECTURE IV.

THE ATONEMENT, ... 95
*The Rev. John H. Elliott, S.T.D., Rector of the
Church of the Ascension, Washington.*

LECTURE V.

THE OFFICE AND WORK OF THE HOLY SPIRIT, . . 121
*The Right Rev. Davis Sessums, D.D., Bishop of
Louisiana.*

LECTURE VI.

GRACE AND THE SACRAMENTAL SYSTEM, ... 155
*By tne Rev. G. H. S. Walpole, M.A., Professor of
Systematic Divinity and Dogmatic Theology
in the General Theological Seminary.*

INTRODUCTION.

WHEN Catholic Dogma is mentioned there are those who ask, is it worth while to spend time in discussing dogma when there is so much work to be done? Give your mind and your labor, they say, to the rescue and help of the wretched and the depraved, the sinful and the unfortunate; go and practise toward them that love which is the fulfilling of the law; but do not waste your energies upon disputations about creeds.

Yet the Church has always occupied itself very largely with dogma, and has strenuously insisted upon the importance of it. With a world to convert, S. Paul filled his letters chiefly with dogma. In the tremendous decline and fall of the Roman empire, and wreck of civilization, the Church dwelt on dogma perpetually, and the Church was in earnest then as now to convert and save the world. In times of reformation not only is righteousness of life emphasized, but the faith of the Church is scrutinized with the keenest criticism. How does it happen that at specially critical times dogma is made so prominent in the Church's life? Inasmuch as it is the peculiar business of the Church, among all the institutions in the world, to teach Christianity, anything that it has uniformly held to be matter of highest importance has a strong *à priori* claim upon our attention. We cannot excuse ourselves for not attending to it by saying that it does not interest us. If it be important it is our duty to attend to it. If it make any difference whether we believe one thing or another, we are bound to find out what the truth is and to maintain it.

In determining whether it is worth while to spend our time in studying and discussing the dogmas of Christianity, we need first to see clearly what Christianity really is. If it were merely a system of conduct, or a system of conduct and worship, much might fairly be said in disparagement of creeds and theology. The fulfilling of the law is love to God and love to man ; why trouble ourselves with anything more ? A popular expression of the day is that Christianity is a life and not a doctrine; therefore, it is urged, let us devote all our energies to right living and not mind the disputations of the schools.

But this view misses the essence of Christianity, and perceives in it simply one among other great religions of mankind. Those are merely systems of conduct and worship, the best methods that men were able to devise for winning that favor of superior beings which has been universally understood by the human mind to be necessary for the attainment of happiness. They are the mature products of that wisdom which men gained from the tree of knowledge of good and evil, while as yet they had found no way to pass the angel who guarded with flaming sword the tree of life. As systems of conduct they are, in some instances at least, highly successful. Some of them might have been refined and purified and have served well enough as a rule of conduct; but our Lord refused to adopt any existing system, because His aim was not merely to promote conduct and worship, but also, and chiefly, to impart to men the gift that He came to bring, the gift of life. This object is plainly declared in the Scriptures: as S. Paul says, "The gift of God is eternal life." "This is the record," says S. John, "that God hath given unto us eternal life, and this life is in His Son." Christ says, "For this cause came I into the world, that they might have life;" and "He that hath the Son hath life; he that hath not the Son of God hath not life."

How to gain eternal life has ever been

and is the chief concern of man. Until Christ came it was sought everywhere in the light of man's knowledge of good and evil, and the only way that man had ever known was the way of righteousness, the only righteous guide conscience. As far as it went the law of conscience did indeed point men in the right direction, for it pointed toward that conduct which is according to the law of love, though uncertainly and vaguely. But the experience of mankind during many ages and in many lands gradually convinced them that something more was necessary. They came to perceive that few if any were able to practise righteousness effectually. The verdict of the thoughtful and wise was that there is none that is righteous, no not one. Moreover, the instinct that craved the support of everlasting arms to uphold human weakness in the storms and crashes of existence was not satisfied. The gods were capricious, and so unreliable that men came to deny that there were any gods.

The instinct that craves sympathy and love found no response. Plainly something was lacking in the various systems of righteousness practised by mankind. Conduct based upon knowledge of good and evil was not saving the world, was not securing eternal life for man.

Christ disclosed what before was lacking, and what men had not been able to discover for themselves. He confirmed the conviction that eternal life is not inherent in human nature and is not acquired by conduct, and showed that it appertains to God only, and must be conveyed from God to each individual in particular. His Gospel is that God hath given us eternal life, offering it to all men, and providing means by which every man has opportunity to make the gift his own.

But that this is not a single simple fact is evident upon slight consideration. Where is that life situated? Where is its source? Where, in the language of the primeval metaphor, is the tree on which it grows? How does it get into us? It is not gained by keeping the law of righteousness, even with the selling of all that one has and giving to the poor, as Christ declared when He bade a seeker after eternal life to follow Him. What did that mean? Not simply to walk in His company over the difficult roads of Palestine; not merely to follow His example of righteous conduct: beyond these things it meant that to gain the gift of life he must lose his own life. And what is this mystery of losing life to gain life? In the Sacrifice of Calvary, where the Son of Man gave up His life in pain, this mystery is elucidated. But what is the explanation? Then, having got life are we sure to keep it? How shall we keep it?

All these, and many more, inquiries meet us as soon as we ask ourselves what are the facts about this gift of life. What we want is facts, not conjectures. If we can only speculate about them we should have known as much if Christ had not come. But Christ has revealed the facts. They were not stated by Him in the form of an edict, as the ten commandments were written on slabs of stone, but they were imparted, from time to time, to the men whom He chose to receive His teaching; and the Church was created for the purpose, among other things, of perpetuating and disseminating this teaching.

The accurate statements of the facts so taught are called dogmas.

Considering now what dogmas are, the disparagement of dogmatic teaching—that is, the teaching of these facts, which Christ revealed, touching the way to get eternal life—implies either a doubt that God has revealed to us the way of life or an inability to appreciate its importance. In either case the necessity for dogmatic teaching is evident. For these facts cannot be ignored. If we get the gift of eternal life by being united with God, clearly we do not make it for ourselves by doing righteousness. The law of that life indeed constrains us to love God and man, and to do the works of love, and we cannot retain the gift unless, in some measure, we live by its law: but natural life and knowledge of good and evil are the conditions for the practice of righteousness, and sufficed for all the virtue of the ancient world; yet the world without Christ and without the gift of life tended to destruction until He came and revealed the gift.

In these lectures the Church Club believes that the right reverend and reverend lecturers have rendered no small service to the Church by stating so lucidly the fundamental facts of Christianity, as they have been revealed to and taught by the Catholic Church, the witness and keeper of the truth. To these learned bishops and priests the Church Club now expresses its own profound obligation.

Catholic Dogma: Its Nature and Obligations.

LECTURE I.
CATHOLIC DOGMA: ITS NATURE AND OBLIGATIONS.

THE RT. REV. A. N. LITTLEJOHN, D.D., LL.D.
Cantab.,
Bishop of Long Island.

Before entering upon the discussion, I have two general remarks to make. (1) I shall speak to believers in the Church's claim to the possession of definite and certain knowledge of the essentials of the faith which it was commissioned to teach. As for unbelievers, whose doubts and objections cover not merely this claim of the Church, but also anterior questions leading up to it, even the existence of God and the possibility of His Incarnation and Revelation to man —they must be left to the wider range of evidence and argument for Christianity itself.

(2) Let it be understood once for all that Catholic dogma does not *fix* a limit to the operations of reason in dealing with divine truth. It simply asserts the *existence* of such a limit *already fixed* in the constitution of nature. God

himself in creating things as we *find* them; not dogma, which simply *describes* them, is responsible for the *fences* of which modern reason so bitterly complains.

My subject is not dogma in general and as popularly applied to all formulated religious truth, but Catholic dogma, which, because it is Catholic, is restricted to Christian verities which bear the mint-stamp of the whole Body of Christ. A dogma to be Catholic must have these three essential, invariable notes.

(1) It must be a truth positively and definitely stated.

(2) It must have directly or by necessary inference, the sure warrant of Holy Scripture.

(3) It must be a truth which has been duly attested by the undivided Church speaking through an Œcumenical Council, and subsequently accepted everywhere and by all in Christendom. Such, briefly, are the signs and notes of Catholic Dogma. Taken together, they sufficiently explain its nature.

But if such be the nature of Catholic dogma, why is it obligatory? The main point and emphasis of the subject are involved in the answer to this question. Obviously the first and chief ground of obligation to accept Catholic dogma is the authority of Holy Scripture on whose warrant it rests, and the authority of the Church constituted and ordained by its Divine Head to be the supreme witness and interpreter of Holy Scripture. These are not two kinds of authority, but rather two aspects of the same authority— even that of the Holy Ghost, equally the inspirer and guide of those who at sundry times and in divers manners composed the written record of God's Revelation to man, and of the living Church appointed to be the keeper and witness of that record. The promise of Divine guidance was not more certainly given in the one case than in the other. In both cases the promise came from the same source, and in both it has been fulfilled through the same instrumentality. The precise measure of the guidance in either case is an idle question. It is enough to know that in each it was sufficient for the end to be attained. For if it was necessary that God should speak to man by successive revelations which were to be made matters of permanent record, it was scarcely less necessary that He should provide a witness and keeper of the record. God anticipated what experience has proved, viz., that we need not only the truth, but also in organic connection with the truth an incorporated and living witness of the truth which would voice its meaning, not as each individual reason might apprehend it, but rather as the divinely guided universal reason of humanity would apprehend it. Through the Holy

Spirit, God in Christ gave the whole of saving truth to the whole of humanity, and the only divinely authorized and final interpreter of this saving truth is the Holy Spirit speaking through the whole of regenerated humanity—even the very Body of Christ which is His Church.

I have said that Catholic dogma is obligatory because it rests upon the twofold authority of Holy Scripture and of the Church as the pillar and ground of the truth. But this twofold authority may be reduced to the yet more simple and ultimate authority of Christ Himself, who, as the eternal Word made flesh and dwelling among us, was, and is, and ever shall be "the truth" as well as "the way and the life." As such He is declared by Holy Scripture to be "the author and finisher of our faith." But if Christ be the author of our faith, then is the substance of what we believe in Him and of Him; and if He be the finisher of our faith, then do the essential articles of our faith derive not only their substance, but also their form, either directly from Him, or indirectly from instrumentalities duly appointed by Him to complete in this regard what He began—even the Scriptures as the record of His Mediatorial work, the Holy Ghost who was to bring all things He had taught to the mind of the Church, and the Church itself as the embodied historic witness of His continuous presence among men. If this be true, then it follows that every dogma which can prove its derivation from the concurrent action of these three witnesses to the mind of Christ can justly claim not only to be Catholic, but to be a veritable transcript of the mind of Christ. For what our Lord said in His own person and what He said through channels of His own selection, are all of one piece as to substance, form, and authority.

In these days of unsettled and contradictory teaching as to the authenticity and genuineness of considerable portions of the Sacred Writings, and as to the true meaning of other portions admitted to be authentic and genuine; and also as to many fundamental matters affecting the being and constitution of the Church—surely it is a great comfort that we are able to trace the foundation of Catholic dogma down to the bed-rock of the authority of our eternal Prophet, Priest, and King, Jesus Christ, who is Lord over all, the same yesterday, to-day, and forever. But to return to the Scriptures and the Church in virtue of whose authority, as commonly cited, Catholic dogma may righly claim to be binding, there are some points to be considered which, if not new, are always important to remember whenever the theme now before us is under discussion. Catholic dogma tightens or loosens its hold on many minds according to the prevailing fashion of religious inquiry and criticism—a fashion which, like other fashions in every-day life, never continues long in one stay. Just now the Scriptures are being tried as by fire. With some their authority in all save morals seems to be on the decline. With others the difficulty and uncertainty in reaching settled and definite conclusions by the inductive or exegetical method of study appear to be growing more and more formidable. Not a few critics and scholars, working on their own individual lines under the influence of the new learning and of the renaissance theology, set forth with increasing boldness their doubts as to whether or no the New Testament Scriptures exhibit any real traces of a divinely authorized organization of the Church; and further, as to whether or no the formulated dogmatic teaching largely introduced by Nicene Christianity had any adequate warrant in the recorded teaching of our Lord and His Apostles. The drift of the so-called advanced criticism seems to be toward not merely the disparagement, but the elimination from the Scriptures of the material of dogmatic teaching; and to find in them only duties, sentiments, aspirations which are sufficiently expressed by a creedless faith, a creedless worship, a creedless hope of eternal life, and a creedless spiritual society. The transition from such views of the Holy Scriptures to like ones of the

Church is easy and natural. The logic, the criticism, the speculative, individualistic temper of mind that issue in such low estimates of the authority and value of Holy Writ make quick work with the authority of the Church on all matters of dogma. In this widespread tendency of our time we have one of the fruits of the popular but philosophically false axiom that nothing is true, nothing is obligatory that does not prove itself to be so to the individual mind regarded as the ultimate court of appeal.*

As the limits of this discourse will compel me to drop many links in the chain of argument, I shall assume the Divine authority of the Scriptures

---

* Protagoras, the best known of the Athenian sophists, was the first to assert as a principle of philosophy, that "Man is the measure of all things." "Just as each thing appears to each man, so it is to him." All truth is relative. He taught this as a necessary corollary from the doctrine of sensation as the source of knowledge. "Man the measure of all things" is the dominant principle—the distinctive characteristic of modern Rationalism in all its criticisms and judgments on the truth of Revealed Religion.

Maurice in his "Kingdom of Christ" shows how this principle works among a large number of Christian people.

"Protestants say that every truth is to be realized by each man for himself, and that when a certain number of individuals have been made conscious of the same truth, they are to meet together and have fellowship in the profession of it; they have never effectually taught men that there are truths appertaining to them as men, which do not depend for their reality upon our consciousness of them, but are the grounds on which the consciousness must rest" (vol. i., p. 193).

as a necessary constituent of Catholic dogma, and will pass on at once to speak of the Divine authority of the Church—the second necessary constituent of Catholic dogma. I do so, not because the latter is of more importance, but simply because there are so many who accept the authority of the written record, and yet deny the authority of the Church. Let me, then, ask you to recall some of the facts—not opinons or speculations—that establish and explain the office of the Church in the evolution and formulation of Catholic dogma. Let it be granted that the Holy Scriptures contain all things necessary to salvation; yet with the light thrown upon the subject by all Christian history, it must also be granted that in order to be assured of a correct statement of these necessary things it is equally needful to have the testimony of a living and continuous witness ordained of Christ, and therefore possessed of authority transcending that of any individual judgment, which shall set forth in their due proportion and in their vital connection with other revealed truths these same necessary things. Always and everywhere to be remembered, this fact has now a special force. For several generations after the Reformation the favorite shibboleth with multitudes was "the Bible, and the Bible only, the religion of Protestants"—a cry that was meant to affirm that the

Bible is its own sufficient witness and interpreter, and that there is and càn be no need to go outside of it for a certain knowledge of its meaning. The first shattering blow to this once popular watchword came from the unsettling and contra- dictory handling of the Scriptures by rival schools of learned interpreters, which had been nursed into power by an ultra use of the private judgment principle*—every man his own inter- preter. The fruits of this principle have now a bitter taste throughout Christendom, and the one chiefly characteristic religious movement of the time—that for the restoration of Christian unity—is at once a protest and a reaction against them. It is now generally conceded that there must have been something radically wrong in a method of arriving at truth whose logical result was the vast brood of modern sects.

---

* What is said here is not intended to question the right and duty of *private judgment*, properly understood. It is the duty of every Christian to search the Scriptures in order to learn from them God's will. Yet this does not weaken, far less supersede, the obligation of individuals to defer to the judgment of the whole Church; nor does it deprive the Church of its inherent right to form a judgment. As has been well said, " It is the duty of every citizen to acquaint himself with the laws of his country and to en- deavor to render them an intelligent obedience; yet this does not take away from a competent tribunal the right of pronouncing judgment according to those laws;" nor, it may be added, does it relieve the citizen from the obligation to accept and obey such judgment when it has been duly pronounced.

But a still more telling blow to this notion—every man for himself in dealing with God's Word—was yet to come from the aggressive school of the new criticism. The great multitude who had been reared under the influence of the maxim "the Bible alone the religion of Protestants," have not now, under the encroachments of this criticism, where to lay their heads. Rightly or wrongly this new criticism has so far breached the old tradition about the plenary and verbal inspiration of the Scriptures, and especially about the authorship, composition, and chronology of certain books of the Sacred Canons as to have quite swept away the once unchallenged idolatry of the text of Scripture. The effect of all this has been to consign to the bats and owls the old cry about the sufficiency of a book religion, and to substitute for it another which puts the emphasis of trust not in what the Book says, but in what the personal Christ says—thus pushing back the ground of belief from the written record to the personality of Christ. But here—assuming that there are only two factors in the field—the historic record of Christ's teaching and the individual interpreter of that teaching, a new crux presents itself. For now the question emerges, Who and what was the Christ? What think ye of Him? A large number of private judgment critics differ about the answer to this question just as radically as they differed about the meaning of other facts and teachings of the Holy Scriptures. And so it has come to pass that multitudes to-day are doubting whether the Christ whom they are to accept is the Christ of the Gospels as set forth in the creed of Nicea, or the Christ of any one of the four great heresies,* or the Christ evolved from the rationalistic amalgam of modern speculation. It is before the irresistible pressure of these facts that the larger part of the sober and thoughtful Christianity of the day is fast retreating once more to the solid ground of Catho-

---

* " There are but four things which concern to make complete the whole state of our Lord Jesus Christ: his deity, his manhood, the conjunction of both, and the distinction of the one from the other being joined in one. Four principal heresies there are which in those things have withstood the truth. Arians, by banding themselves against the deity of Christ; Apollinarians by maiming and misinterpreting that which belongeth to his human nature; Nestorians, by rending Christ asunder and dividing him into two persons; the followers of Eutychus, by confounding in his person those natures which they should distinguish. In four words, *truly, perfectly, indevisably, distinctly;* the first applied to his being God, and the second to his being man, the third to his being of both One, and the fourth to his still continuing in that one Both; we may fully, by way of abridgment, comprise whatever antiquity hath at large handled either in declaration of Christian belief, or in refutation of the aforesaid heresies, within the compass of which four heads I may truly affirm that all heresies which touch but the person of Jesus Christ, whether they have risen in these late years or in any age heretofore, may be with great facility brought to confine themselves." Hooker's " Ecclesiastical Polity," bk. v., ch. liv., sect. 10.

lic dogma—the Holy Scriptures as voiced and formulated by the Catholic Church in the ages of its unbroken unity.

With these preliminary considerations fixed in our thoughts, we are now prepared to pass in review the grounds of the Church's authority and competency for the task of setting forth the faith once delivered. And here let it be remembered that whatever the extent of this authority and competency, precisely the same is the extent of our obligation to accept what she teaches out of God's Word. Whence, then, and what is the Church? It were attempting more than my space will allow to quote in detail all that the Scriptures tell us on the subject. Their language throbs with a profoundly mystical, but logically real, meaning. Reason, feeling, imagination are tasked to the uttermost to express the depth and intensity of their conception of the Body of Christ. If anything in them is declared to be absolutely of God and not of man, it is the Church. It was the fulfilment of his purpose, the creation of his will, the revelation of his wisdom and love. The Church's life is the embodied life of God in Christ speaking by the Holy Ghost. The Church's faith is the truth of God in Christ made known to man through the Holy Ghost. The Church's moral power, when at its best, is the moral power of the perfect righteousness of God in Christ commended to every man's conscience by the Holy Ghost. If it be a body of many members, it is one with its Head. If it be a growth, it is one with the grower. If it be a building, it is one with the builder. If it be the bride of Christ, it is eternally one with the Bridegroom. It is not a construction put together piece by piece even by the Divine will, but rather in its ultimate idea a spiritual generation and outbirth of the Godhead who was made flesh and dwelt among us. Given the fact of the Incarnation, and the Church followed as a vital organic sequence. But if Christ as the Head of the Church could so imbue it with His own personality as to make it the continued manifestation of Himself among men, it is only natural to expect that He would so order its organization and work as to show forth in them through the ages all His essential gifts and functions—even His power of regeneration and santification by His Word and Sacraments —His power to teach and rule—His power as the logos to give enduring form to the truth. It was in fact the Church's possession of these several powers by derivation and commission that imparted to it its supreme authority under Christ as the keeper and witness of what had been taught by Himself and His Apostles. Now let it be understood that, in the many references in the Scriptures to this authority as an indubitable fact, we are to look not so much for explicit directions for its exercise, as for recognition of its existence and of its practical use in formulating the truth committed to its keeping. The Church is made up of men, and yet it is so made of men as to be the Body of Christ, the very habitation of His Spirit. It is at once divine and human; "certainly infallible because of the divine and as certainly infallible because of the union of the human with the divine—the human not inerrable in itself, but only as the organ and manifestation of the divine." The human is so taken up into the living Christ and permeated by His Spirit that, though its voice continues to be human, its message is divine; and, because divine, at once infallible and universal. This view of the Church is a necessary inference from the Incarnation. Christ became man that He might mediate between man and God. He did so mediate during His personal ministry on earth, and afterward through the Church which is His Body, and, because His Body, the continuation of His mediatorial work in history. It was to the Apostles and through them to the universal Episcopate, the official representative of His Body, that Christ said, "Lo, I am with you alway even unto the end of the world;"* "The Comforter, the

---

* St. Matthew, 28: 20.

Holy Ghost, whom the Father will send in my Name, he shall teach you all things, and bring all things to your remembrance, whatsoever I have said unto you."* And then, as if to show how completely the members of the Body share all things with the Head, there is His prayer, " I in them and thou in me, that they may be made perfect in one."† How these promises were regarded—how the Church, as deriving upon itself the authority of its Head as the keeper and witness of the truth, was understood at the very sunrise of its being and amid the freshly knit bonds of Christ and His Body, we have ample proof in the infallibility assumed as matter of course by the Synod of Jerusalem, at which all the Apostles were present. That "it seemed good to the Holy Ghost and to us" was esteemed the sufficient warrant for promulgating its decrees as certain truth. It was the whole Church that spoke in that first Council; and whenever, in subsequent Councils, the whole Church has spoken substantially the same claim has been made and in the same way. The guiding presence of the Holy Ghost has, in every case, been accounted the determining factor in the work done; and no dogma has ever been reckoned Catholic that did not bear the seal of the Spirit of all truth as affixed by the synodical action of the Church, attesting

---

* St. John, 14:26.   † St. John, 17:23.

thereby the fundamental rule of Catholic consent—*semper, ubique et ab omnibus*. Strangely enough there is, in some quarters, a disposition to drop out the *semper* as a necessary element in a truly Catholic consent. It is claimed that a dogma held everywhere and by all at any given time implies that it has always been held. This breach in the logic of the ancient rule seems intended to make room for the introduction to-day as Catholic dogmas of what aforetime were only matters of opinion—a breach, be it remembered, through which the Latin Church seeks to drive the Vatican decrees of 1854 and 1870. And yet the rule as thus mutilated would not benefit Rome unless she could first establish her claim to be the Catholic Church—a thing impossible. It is of the last importance that we stand fast upon the ancient rule in its integrity. Not merely general consent at any one time is demanded, but also continuous consent embracing the witness of the undivided Church, and, as far as may be, that of the faithful in all the following ages. Inerrancy is not the gift of any individual Church, national or provincial, but of the Church as a whole. In the words of our XIX. Article, "As the Church of Jerusalem, Alexandria, and Antioch hath erred, so also the Church of Rome hath erred, not only in their living and manner of ceremonies, but also in matters of faith." But further, if the Church Catholic be *indefectible*, as our Lord declared it to be, when He said, "the gates of hell shall never prevail against it," then it follows that there must be a sense in which it is *infallible*. For if it is never to fail it must be endowed with all power and authority needful to the preservation of the truth on which its own life depends. But the preservation of the truth involves a power and authority for defining the truth against errors which the Church's Divine Head alone can give. In only two ways would it be possible for the Church to fail. It might perish by the apostasy or death of all its members, or it might perish by the lapse of all Christians into heresy. But in neither of these ways can it perish, if the promise of its Head be true. Its indefectibility is an established supernatural fact, but it is so only to the extent that it is able to maintain an infallible guardianship over the revealed verities which are the fountain of its life and the charter of its work. Still further, if the Church, like its Lord, be in all its essentials the same yesterday, to-day, and forever, then as it began on the day of Pentecost, so in respect of these essentials it has continued to this day. And since it does not claim to have received any new revelation of truth, so neither can it claim authority to add any new dogma to the faith once delivered to the saints. The infallibility of the Catholic Church does not, as falsely claimed for itself by the Latin Church, involve the power to introduce new saving truth, or to translate pious opinions into obligatory dogmas; but is restricted to defining and promulgating what has been held from the beginning. The Church is an infallible witness and keeper of an original deposit, not an infallible discoverer of what was before unknown. If what God has revealed seems to grow, the growth is not in itself, but simply in our human apprehension of it. The mind of man grows, not God's message.

And just here, as another important step in the argument, it should be understood that we cannot properly appreciate the office of the Church as the keeper and expounder of the Catholic faith unless we give due weight to the following well-attested historic fact. The origin and first establishment of Christianity were by the preaching of living men commissioned to proclaim it. There is a vague notion that Christianity was taken from the New Testament. This is historically untrue. Christianity in fact was widely extended through the world before the New Testament was written, and its several books were successively addressed to various bodies of Christian believers, who already possessed the faith of Christ in its integrity.

"When, indeed, God ceased to inspire persons to write these books, and when they were all collected by the Church in what we call the New Testament, the already existing faith of the Church derived from oral teaching was tested by comparison with the Inspired record; and it henceforth became the standing rule of the Church that nothing should be received as necessary to salvation which could not stand that test." But still though thus tested by the New Testament, Christianity is not taken from it; for it existed before it. What, then, was the Christianity that was thus established before the New Testament writings appeared? Have we any record of it as it existed before the New Testament became the sole authoritative standard? I answer: the creeds of the Christian Church are the record of it. That is precisely what they purport to be; not documents taken from the New Testament, but documents transmitting to us the faith as it was held from the beginning—"the faith as it was preached by inspired men, before inspired men put forth any writings;" the Faith once and for all delivered to the saints. Accordingly, you will find that this Church in her VIII. Article does not ground the affirmation that the creeds ought to be "thoroughly received and believed;" on the fact "that they were taken out of the New Testament (which they were not); but on the fact that they may be proved by most certain warrants of Holy Scripture." The Church, then, was first the keeper and witness of the creeds containing all essential truths; and afterward the keeper and witness of the New Testament writings, by which in the generations to come these creeds were to be tested and proved; and she is divinely declared to be the pillar and ground of the truth because she is the keeper and witness of both. These indisputable facts go a long way toward explaining and establishing the peculiar authority which attaches to Catholic consent—the settled and determinate voice of the whole Church in the formulation and promulgation of Divine truth.* But whatever this authority in kind or in degree, in accordance with a fundamental rule of Catholic practice, it has always been exercised through General Councils. It is important, therefore, to have clear views not only of the authority itself, but also of the organ through which it has spoken. Now though in the strict sense of the terms general, universal, Œcumenical are the same, yet the term Œcumenical has been declared by usage to mean " a

---

* " So complete is the historical acceptance of the creeds, and their consecration in the consciousness of the Church, that there is at least as clear a presumption that we are uncatholic in differing from them as there would be that we were unscientific if we dissented from the most universally accepted faiths of science."— R. C. MOBERLY, *Lux Mundi*, p. 243.

General Council, lawful, approved, and received by all the Church." A council may be general without being lawful; to be general, all the bishops of the world should be summoned to it, and no one excluded save the heretical and excommunicated. This rule was absolutely observed in none of the so-called General Councils, and only a minority of bishops sat in most of them. To be lawful and truly Œcumenical it is necessary that all that occurs should be done regularly (which was not the case with some of the General Councils), and that the Church at large should accept its decrees, as was done with those of the Councils of Nice, Constantinople, Ephesus and Chalcedon. That a General Council be accepted, it is not required that all the faithful individually considered acquiesce in its action. It suffices for the purpose that all branches of the Church do so in their corporate capacity.* We know that there have been Councils general in their convocation, but not so in their acts and results. It follows, then, that "while the Church is in her present divided condition, local churches must confine themselves to making local decrees. Such local decrees may hereafter, either by the approval of the whole Church become part of

---

* On the authority of General Councils, see Palmer "On the Church," part iv., chap. 8 ; also Browne "On the Twenty-first Article."

the Church's living teaching, or undergo a certain modification in order to secure such approval." There is no agreement as to the number of truly Œcumenical Councils. "The Anglican Church, in some of her documents, refers to St. Gregory's four; in others, to six. The Greek Church holds eight; though Barlaam in A.D. 1339, treating with Benedict XII., mentions only six.* The Latin Church does not agree with itself on the subject —some of its doctors counting twenty-one, and some considerably less."† Though I have spoken

---

* Palmer, vol. ii., p. 203 ; Bp. Forbes, p. 300.

† In view of what has been said, it may be asked of what practical use are Universal Synods ; and what authority are we to assign them ? Certainly these are pertinent questions when it is admitted, as it must be, that no one of the four or six so-called Œcumenical Councils actually conformed to the conditions declared to be necessary to the complete constitution and work of an Œcumenical Council ; *i. e.*, that all bishops in regular standing must be duly summoned, that at least a large majority must be present, and that all things must be lawfully and regularly done.

The answer is (and we give it in the words of Browne and substantially of Beveridge and Forbes on the Articles): "So far as General Councils speak the language of the Universal Church and are accredited by the Church, so far they have the authority inherent in the Church of deciding in controversies of faith. Now we can only know that they speak the language of the Church when their decrees meet with universal acceptance by the whole Church. Every General Council which has received this stamp to its decisions may be esteemed to speak the language of the Universal Church ; and, as in most cases, the judgment of the Universal Church could not otherwise be elicited, therefore we must admit their importance and necessity. Now the first six, or, at least, the first four Genat large of the Church's relation to the Holy Scriptures, it may be well to say a word about the specific relation to them that General Coun-

eral Councils, have received this sanction of universal consent to their decisions. Their decrees were sent round throughout the Christian world and were approved by all the national churches of Europe, Asia, and Africa. The errors condemned by them were then, and ever have been, accounted heresies; and the creeds set forth by them have been acknowledged, reverenced, and constantly repeated in the liturgy by every orthodox church from that time to this. Thus, then, the true General Synods have received an authority which they had not in themselves." I may venture to add that the underlying essential point to be determined is not the precise amount of authority to be attributed to General Councils, but the existence of such authority in the Church in some form, as enabled it to set forth, whenever required, obligatory definitions of the faith.

A question has been raised as to the authority of conciliary decisions, because the ages of councils were uncritical ages. It is enough to say that they were not convened for purposes of criticism; but to collect, harmonize, and formulate the testimony of all branches of the Church as to its own original deposit of faith. The issues they were called to decide were issues of historic fact, whose final appeal was to the witness, from the beginning, of the continuous and universal consciousness of the Church. What we understand by criticism, with its complex apparatus of investigation and its professional experts, would have been out of place in the councils. The qualities needed were in the main those which belong to an intelligent, clear-headed, honest jury, whose chief business it is to give a verdict upon the facts presented. The councils declared the meaning and force of certain absolutely proven facts, and the only pertinent question is whether they were right or wrong in their judgment. There is no doubt that they were sure what they meant, and just as little that they expressed with perfect clearness what they meant.

cils have always maintained. The significant symbol of this relation was a copy of the Holy Gospels placed on a throne in the midst of the assembly as the type of the guiding presence of the Holy Ghost. It has always been held that it is the duty of a Council to declare what has been the faith from the beginning, not to put forth new objects of belief. It might, on any given matter, develop implicit into explicit faith; but it was required to show that the matter so developed was a portion of the original deposit and revelation. But it is a fact, of which ecclesiastical history furnishes abundant evidence, that General Councils may err and sometimes have erred in things pertaining to God. "The inerrancy of a council can never be guaranteed at the moment. The value of a council is tested by its after reception by the Church. Synods of very limited numbers in obscure places have by after reception assumed the weight of an Œcumenical Council; as, for example, that of Orange on the question of grace: on the other hand, one act of the holiest of all Councils—that of Jerusalem in the Acts of the Apostles—in the matter of things strangled, has in the West become obsolete. Again, some canons of a council are accepted and some are rejected. Discipline also may change so that in respect of disciplinary decrees there is not only an after verdict by the living

Church, but there is also in operation a corrective process in things non-essential so far as they affect the well-being of the Church."* But it has always been held that in the case of dogma touching any fundamental verity of the faith the decision of an approved Œcumenical Council settles the matter for all time.

Just at this point we are confronted by a fact of solemn moment. The last undisputed General Council was held at the close of the seventh century (680). Is it true, then, that the Church's only duly accredited organ for defining and formulating truth has been in abeyance for 1200 years, or since the great schism between the East and West? If it be true, the consequences are not so grave as some would have us think. The suspended exercise of one form of the Church's authority does not involve the suspension of her authority in other forms. In spite of this she may still do her work as the *ecclesia docens*, and in various ways enjoy the benefits of the Spirit's guidance into all truth necessary to salvation; still it is, indeed, a startling fact that her plenary power for deciding controversies should have been for so many centuries powerless. What inward lesions and outward assaults may have come upon her, because of this dormant function only her own eternal Head can

---
* Bp. Forbes "On the Articles," p. 299.

surely know. Certain it is that, while schism continues to do its will upon the torn body, the power of inerrancy inherent only in the united whole cannot be set in motion. All that has been decreed in any one of the hundred parts is liable to revision, and the guidance so freely promised to the Universal Episcopate must be greatly narrowed as to its present use. It brings little comfort to be reminded by those who study all history from the standpoint of philosophy, that, bad as the case is, it has at least saved the Church from "the danger of over definition of the faith," and has cleared the field of Christian thought of all barriers and fences not absolutely necessary.

But, however we may lament this arrested power of the Church, she still remains a witness to the truth, even if for the time she has ceased to declare infallibly fresh truth. If she cannot sanction new dogmas, she can testify to the old; and the old, be it remembered, cover all truth essential to salvation, or needful for the perfection of individual spiritual life. With this we must be content while schisms last. What a motive in all this to labor and pray for the return of unity! May God hasten it in His own time and way, building up again the breaches in the Temple not made with hands, " bringing together, in the fulness of their proper organic life, the scattered limbs of His Mystical Body and reviving the heavenly song of Pentecostal Unity." Then and not till then will be heard again the long silent voice, and will be seen once more in their divine beauty the Urim and the Thummim of an infallible prophetic inspiration. The argument thus far for the binding validity of Catholic dogma has been based upon principles that lie at the root of Christian theology. Let me now, so far as time will allow, complete the argument by an appeal to the Church's experience. Of all the lessons taught by this experience none is more positive than this: viz., that without a dogmatic faith (always Catholic in its fundamentals) the Church cannot fulfil its normal functions, or accomplish the primary ends of its existence.

(1) The Church was ordained and constituted to be a teaching body; but it cannot teach unless it have something to teach—something that has *form* as well as substance. The truths of Revelation, like all other truths, must have their terms and definitions; the moment we begin to treat them as the subject matter of instruction. Their mutual limitations must be explained. Apparent contradiction must not be allowed to displace either one of two truths which our logic is too narrow to reconcile. Truths which are to be taught must be stated;

but to state them is to define and formulate them. This must be done not only for didactic uses, but equally so to guard them against error. For, if the truth have no settled boundaries, it is defenceless against heresy. Heresy is impossible where truth is undefined. But defined truth is positive truth, and positive truth in religion is only another name for Christian dogma. If, then, the Church is to teach out of God's Word, and it is a necessary part of its commission to do so, then it must determine what, and how, and when it is to teach. But this it cannot do unless it give form to the knowledge it would communicate; and if it do this, it must have creeds, and if these, then dogmas. (2) Again, experience has proved that a creedless Church cannot be a Missionary Church. Potentially all dogmas that have any claim upon us were involved in the Saviour's command, " Go ye, therefore, and teach all nations, baptizing them in the Name of the Father, and of the Son, and of the Holy Ghost." Without a positive message to deliver, the Church, whatever its energy and enthusiasm, cannot cope with the powers of the world, far less gather to its standard hostile races or supplant false religions. The moment it begins to substitute sentiment, or vague notions of truth for a definite creed, it begins also to wither and weaken in its missionary power. What was true of St. Paul and of those who wrought with him in the Apostolic age is true now. Whatever else he held back when he wrote to the Romans and Ephesians, the Galatians and Colossians, or when he preached to the wise men of Athens, he did not withhold the dogmatic verities of the faith. He did not think his duty done by exhorting them to be devout and righteous, and to unite in hymns and prayers, if they would unite in nothing else. Christ Jesus, indeed, was the burden of his tongue and pen, but it was Christ Jesus explained and defined. St. Paul's Christ was a person, and to save Him from evaporating into a myth among the generations of men, the historic fact was developed and formulated into articles of belief. So the Church preaches Christ to-day, and it is only as it does so that it can go forth among the nations conquering and to conquer.

(3) Still again, the Church was commissioned to act as the custodian, through all time, of a certain type of spiritual life in its own body and in its individual members. This type is spread out in the Word of God and in the lives of prophets, apostles and confessors. It is repeated in every page of Christian history, and can be discerned to-day amid all differences in the great company of the faithful throughout all the world. It has been disturbed and infringed chiefly by two tendencies within the Church—the one cropping

out in a dead orthodoxy, the other in a spiritual mysticism; the one eliminating life from dogma, the other dogma from life. The latter is our danger. The spirit and fashion of the time are with it. The religion of the day is mostly one of affinity and feeling, not of knowledge or principle. Christian mystics and latitudinarian sentimentalists dread nothing so much as a dogmatic faith. It seems not to have dawned upon them that a creedless religion is simply a body without bones, a bridge without abutments, and that it is impossible to conceive of a confession which has nothing to confess—a faith which has nothing to be believed. It is, then, the voice of experience as well the voice of God's Word and of right reason that the Church can hope to maintain the true life of God in itself and in the individual soul only as it adheres to a positive faith.

(4) Again, it is certain that the Church was intended to preserve and transmit the distinctive characteristics of Christian morality. Natural morality has no dogmatic foundation. Christian morality is Christian chiefly because it has such a foundation. Every attempt to separate the moral from the dogmatic teaching of the Church has failed. No man can put asunder what God has joined together; and for this reason among others: no man can tell where the one be-

gins and the other ends. Doctrine and duty, what we believe and what we do, are but different sides of the same divine message and form one and the same organic whole. The moral law, the truth as it is in Jesus, the faith which apprehends the truth and the personal duties that germinate from it, are all vital elements of the one Revelation to man. Therefore, it is impossible to teach Christian morals apart from Christian dogma.

(5) Finally, we cannot but believe that the Church was meant so to administer the trusts and affairs of its Divine Charter as to command in every age the sympathy and support of the best culture and intelligence of mankind. This view has, in every generation, had much to do with directing the thought and study, and through these the theology of the Church. Its intellectual activity centres in the work of inculcating and defending its dogmas. On their human side these dogmas bear the impress of its intelligence. They have been shaped by its thought and cast in the mould of its learning. They are its formal answers at the bar of reason to the world's demand for some rational account of its faith. Had the Church only sentiment to cherish and propagate, or only moral duties to inculcate, simply urging men to be good and devout—it would need little intelligence and less mental activity; for its task would be so simple and uniform as to demand but a

small measure of either. Dogmas may be scouted by unbelief, treated with scant respect by the advanced thinkers of the day, or with indifference by their own chosen teachers; but, after all, they are the intellectual bonds which connect the Church with all the highest thinking of the day. And such is the constitution of the Church that it must be strong in its intellectual work, if it would be so in its spiritual work; and, whatever its strength, it all flows on in one current of power.

Such, then, are the nature and obligations of Catholic dogma. If what I have set forth be true, what else shall be said than that he who trifles with the Church's creed assails the vital functions of the Church itself, cripples its power to teach and convert the nations, and weakens its hold on a sound and balanced spiritual life. Is it not true that he who undermines the faith undermines the morality of the Gospel? Does he not attack the hope who attacks the doctrine of Salvation? Are not they in every age to be accounted vicious meddlers with the ordinances of God who magnify practice at the expense of belief, unity of spirit at the cost of unity of faith and order?

The Dogma of the Trinity.

In regard to the lecture on The Trinity, which appears in this volume, it should be stated that the original lecture on that subject was delivered by the Rev. Dr. Shackleford, but after its delivery the manuscript was mislaid. The Rev. Dr. Huntington kindly volunteered to supply this serious loss, and the paper on the subject herein published was prepared by him. It is thus owing to his courtesy in the matter that the course now published is complete.

LECTURE II.

THE REV. WILLIAM REED HUNTINGTON, D.D.,
Rector of Grace Church, New York.

THE DOGMA OF THE TRINITY.

For all people will walk every one in the name of his god, and we will walk in the name of the Lord our God for ever and ever. MICAH iv. 5.

CHRISTENDOM is differentiated from heathendom simply by a better knowledge of what God is like. All other phases of the contrast between the two realms are trivial as compared with this. Doubtless every one of the races of men has some notion of divinity, more or less clearly defined; they are all of them religious, even theological, after their fashion; they "walk every one in the name of his god;" but that which gives the Christian peoples their pre-eminence and puts them in the front of civilization is the fact that they possess a better informed religion, a more enlightened theology, a juster appreciation of what is covered by "the name of their God" than the others have. They not only know God in the sense of being persuaded that He exists, but in some measure they apprehend, even while confessing that they cannot comprehend, His character and His ways. In a word, the difference is a doctrinal difference; the Christian peoples have been the more intelligently taught; there has come into their hands an altogether better tradition of God.

This distinction between knowing and knowing intelligently is familiar enough, for it is emphasized whenever, in any inquiry, the point of accuracy is raised; but the other contrast, namely, that which lies between an *intelligent* and a *perfect* knowledge, is not so often noted. Everybody, in a sense, knows the sun: it is impossible to mistake it for anything else, or anything else for it. But the converse of the proposition may be equally well maintained, namely, that nobody knows the sun; nobody knows it, that is to say, in the sense of being able to explain fully its interior condition, or to make out the secret of its heat-supply. In fact, it may be truthfully said that our ignorance of the sun is vastly more extensive than our acquaintance with it. And yet to belittle on this account the stores of knowledge acquired by aid of the telescope, the spectroscope, and the polariscope is scarcely a creditable thing. What the astronomer of to-day knows about the sun may indeed be very little as compared with what might be known, but it is very much as compared with what the savage knows, or even with what the civilized man of average education knows. This is the justification of pure theology. It is not alleged by the Christian thinker that it is possible to "find out the Almighty unto perfection;" but it is affirmed, and affirmed with confidence, that of the Power throned at the heart of things it has been given us to know more than the mere fact that it exists.

It may be objected to the solar illustration just employed, that being drawn from the natural universe it is inapplicable to such personal relations as Christian theology postulates between the soul and God. And yet it is easy enough to show that this same characteristic of gradation attaches to the kind of knowledge which spirits have of one another. We all feel that we know Cromwell, for example; know him, that is to say, as a person markedly different from all the other persons whose portraits hang in the gallery of our thoughts. On the other hand, there is no one who perfectly knows Cromwell except Cromwell's Maker. Meanwhile, midway, or rather part way between the Almighty's absolute and perfect knowledge of Cromwell and my own faint and dim apprehension of what he was, comes such an acquaintance with the man's personality as was enjoyed by Milton and Fairfax among his contemporaries and by Carlyle and Guizot among his critics. Similarly, in every-day life, how many people we know " by sight " or " by name ; " and yet how few we know intelligently, know in such a way as to be able to predict decisively how they would act if placed in this or that position, subjected to such or such a temptation, weighted with some special task or responsibility or sorrow! Now, it may be laid down as generally true that the more intelligent our knowledge, whether of things or of persons, the more satisfactory it is and the more pleasure it gives us. Other things being equal, the accomplished scholar travels over the globe with infinitely more delight than the chance tourist; and to the eye of the naturalist or the painter many a landscape dull to ordinary observers is brimming over with suggestion. It cannot, therefore, in religion be a matter of indifference whether the object of worship is apprehended with more or with less of intelligence, whether God is known to us as

" Jehovah, Jove, or Lord."

This brings us directly to our subject.

All the theologies that have risen above the level of mere fetichism or sorcery may be comprehensively classed under five heads: (1) Pantheism, (2) Polytheism, (3) Dualism, (4) Monotheism without personal differentiation, and (5) Monotheism with personal differentiation.

To these correspond certain formulas easily

remembered; to wit, the pantheistic "God is the all, and the all is God;" the polytheistic "There are gods many and lords many;" the dualistic "Ormuzd and Ahriman;" the Hebrew "There is one God" (to which the Moslem appends, "and Mahomet is his prophet"); and the Christian "There is one God: Father, Son, and Holy Ghost." It is maintained by the inheritors of the last-named formula that it both recognizes and reconciles all that is true in the other four, while at the same time strenuously exclusive of whatever in them has been found harmful, whether by way of logical issue or of practical result. For example, it is the virtue of pantheism that by distributing deity throughout the universe it literally makes all things everywhere aglow with God, no temple-measurements being thought worthy of His divine Majesty less lofty than the heavens above or narrower than the east is from the west. On the other hand, the vice of pantheism is the confusion which its denial of God's personality brings about between holiness and unholiness. Nature, unfortunately, is not nice in her ethical distinctions. It is true that in the long run her fires and fevers make war against sensual sin, but to the transgression of the wicked she often seems, in individual cases, strangely blind; while upon certain grave offences against righteousness she pronounces no censure at all. The moral philosophy of pantheism sums itself up in the saying, " What Nature dictates, dare to do," a maxim as plausible as it is rhythmical, but which some accepting and acting upon have found themselves in hell.

The Christian theologian concedes, without demur, all that the pantheist has to say concerning the omnipresence of deity, the immanence of God within and throughout both universes, the seen and the unseen; better than this, he carries the war into Africa by demanding the name of any pantheistic author, whether philosopher or poet, who has given worthier utterance in words to this great truth than St. Paul, than Monica the mother of Augustine, than William Wordsworth, Christians every one of them. But this, which is the whole of pantheism, is but the half of what prophets, evangelists, and apostles teach, for these last add to the conception of the divine immanence the further and still grander thought of the divine transcendence, supplementing the dogma "God is everywhere" by the *addendum* "and everywhere the Judge." In polytheism also, as in pantheism, the Christian theologian is frank to recognize a certain measure of truth. The heroes and demigods of polytheism testify, in a blind way, to man's craving after a deity who can meet him on his own ground and be touched by a feeling of his infirmities, some divine Word capable of being "made flesh" and of dwelling among us. The simple barbarians, who named Barnabas "Jupiter" and Paul "Mercury," under the impression that "the gods" had come down to them, witnessed, without knowing it, to their need of the very message these missionaries had come to bring, the tidings that God had "visited His people." Moreover, polytheism deserves credit for the stress it lays on the social phase of the divine existence. The council on Olympus indicates a conviction on the part of the framer or framers of the mythology in which it plays so prominent a part, that even within deity itself there must be scope for what we know as mutuality or fellowship. What measure of recognition Christian theology accords to this demand will be seen later on; for the moment, it is enough to note the point as worth remembering that the classic mythology was practically a deification of society.

But polytheism is found hopelessly wanting both in its physics and its ethics; in its physics, because without an acknowledged archon or head the cosmos is hopelessly unintelligible; in its ethics, because, with a multitude of gods and goddesses who confessedly share man's weaknesses as they share his virtues, there can be no fixed standard of conduct. Sterile of scientific suggestion, and in morals prolific mainly of the bad, polytheism held out against the Christian faith only so long as it was bolstered by brute force.

The third of the inadequate theologies, dualism, is simply polytheism reduced to its lowest terms. The dualistic hypothesis gathers up all the antagonisms and contrarieties to be found anywhere in the universe, and marshals them under the two great heads of a power making for good and a power making for evil. Dualism is a practical surrender of all hope of a final harmony, an ultimate pacification; for if the two kingdoms, that of light and that of darkness, are co-eternal, their dissidence and conflict must also be from everlasting to everlasting, and world without end. This is pessimism but one degree unmoved from its worst.

There remains to be considered monotheism, or the belief that deity has but one source and fount, and that to name two gods is as grave a blasphemy as to name a thousand. This is the doctrine which by aid of Holy Scripture we find ourselves able to trace back as far as the thread of human history runs. At no time has it been held by all, at many times it has been held only by a few, but at all times it has been held by some. If we divest ourselves for a moment of our inherited prepossessions in favor of this faith, and consider how much there is in nature and in human life that seems at first sight to make dead against the monotheistic creed, we cannot but wonder that in days when pantheism, polytheism, and dualism all were strong it should have made out to achieve survival.

In the full daytime of a monotheistic civilization the supremacy of such a faith is easily enough understood; but how as "a light shining in a dark place" it should have made out to glimmer on as it did is explicable most easily upon the theory which assigns the origin of the belief to revelation and the continuance of it to providential care. But while the Bible, taken as a whole, may be regarded as the great record-book of monotheism, it is impossible not to notice a strikingly significant distinction between the Old Testament and the New Testament theologies. The great end and aim of revelation in pre-Christian times seems to have been to stamp ineffaceably upon the mind of man the truth, "There is one God, and there is none other but He." As against pantheism, polytheism, and dualism, this was the witness to be witnessed until the dogma of the divine unity should become to the Church as bone of her bone and flesh of her flesh. This end accomplished—and it took more than "the wisdom of a thousand years" to do it—it became possible to amplify and enrich the doctrine of God without imperilling the integrity of it; possible to show that the divine unity, so strenuously insisted upon in the Law, the Prophets, and the Psalms, was not the mere synonym of singleness, but rather should be conceived of as a unity of that more fruitful type which implies union and communion. In harmony with this view, we note the fact that every stage, epoch, era, crisis, in the progressive revelation of God to man has been marked by the annunciation of a name. Always in Scripture we find "name" used either as significant of the power or as interpretative of the nature of the One whose name it is. The Bible-names, like the chemist's symbols, tell their own story; they are more than mere tags: they supply a genuine analysis, give insight into character, are literally hieroglyphic.

When God appeared to Abraham and laid the foundations of that family covenant which was destined afterward to broaden into the charter of the Holy Catholic Church, the words with which he opened the august interview were these, "I am the Almighty God." It was the communication of a name, a name full of suggestions of majesty and strength. From that time on there was to be no looking backward on Abraham's part to the "gods" which he had left on the other side of the stream. When Moses received at the hand of this same Abraham's God his commission to be the leader of the exodus, there is again the communication of a name—"And God said unto Moses, I AM THAT I AM. And he said, Thus shalt thou say unto the children of Israel, I AM hath sent me unto you." Later in the same document we find these remarkable words: "And God spake unto Moses and said unto him, I am the Lord, and I appeared unto Abraham, unto Isaac, and unto Jacob by the name of God Almighty, but by my name JEHOVAH was I not known to them." Difficult as the interpretation of this passage undoubtedly is, it certainly does illustrate the point that a characteristic feature of God's gradual unveiling of the truth about Himself has been the successive annunciation of names. Just in proportion to men's enlarged knowledge of what God is like has been their need of a new name for Him; and conversely the new name, when announced, has served as finger-post to a still larger knowledge.

When we pass to the New Testament, we find ourselves confronted at the very portals of the Gospel by a new name. St. Mark opens with the words, "The beginning of the Gospel of Jesus Christ, the Son of God." Evidently a fresh revelation is at hand, harbingered as usual by a name. Following this Jesus, and noting with carefulness what He says, we find Him continually speaking of His Father, of Himself, and as His ministry draws toward its end, of One whom He names "the Spirit." His language, with respect to each of these three, is what we know as personal language. He speaks of the "Father" as the One by whom He has been sent into the world; He speaks of "the Spirit" as One whom He Himself will send. Surely if language means anything, language such as this means that here are three predicates. Unless the speaker is trifling with words, it follows necessarily from what He says that the Father is not the Son, that the Son is not the Spirit, and that the Spirit is not the Father. But even though the diversity be conceded, why admit the equality? Why not suppose a hierarchy of powers—the Father the Supreme, the Son a being of second rank, the Spirit tertiary? For the best of reasons, as found in the last recorded words of the Revealer Himself. Jesus Christ, about to part from His apostles, gives them a commission. By an appointment made on the day of the Resurrection they have met in Galilee; they are alone together on a mountain-top; it is a critical moment, the climax of the earthly ministry; now, if ever, is the time for the whole substance of the revelation, which this Christ has come to bring, to be compressed into a sentence, into one memorable word. It is spoken. Jesus says to them: "All authority hath been given unto me in Heaven and on earth. Go ye therefore, and make disciples of all the nations, baptizing them into the name of the Father and of the Son and of the Holy Ghost."* When we remember how intense was the sanctity attached by the Hebrew mind to the first of these three names, "the Father," we see at once that to have coupled with it two others of lesser dignity would have seemed to the disciples the height of blasphemy. Doubtless it startled them to hear this new name enunciated at all; but once heard, it must have become immediately the synonym of deity. It is difficult, indeed, to imagine them, with their exalted notions of the honor due to the name of God, so interpreting their commission as to make it read, "Baptizing them into the name of the Father Everlasting, of a Creature born in time, and of an Influence potent for good." Yet this last is the alternative rendering which those who can see in the dogma of the Trinity nothing better than a metaphysical paradox would have us accept. Thus solemnly enunciated, the Christian Name of God fell on the ear like the morning gun of a new day—"Light has come into the world," men said, and with reason. Yet it was not imagined—for how could it be?—that the new Name would displace and supersede the old. Jesus Christ had not come to reveal a God other than He whom Abraham, Moses, and Isaiah

---

* St. Matt. xxviii. 19, *Revised Version.*

had worshipped, but only to reveal the same God more fully. Some way there must be, if only it could be found, of reconciling the threeness of the new Name with the oneness of the old. The thought that the God of Truth could by any possibility have contradicted himself in these successive unveilings of his countenance was not for a moment to be entertained. This, then, was one of the great questions with which the masterminds of the early Church found themselves compelled to wrestle—How could God be one, and yet also be, as Christ had represented, "Father, Son, and Holy Ghost"? The apostles, in their time, handled the problem in ways that we should call practical and devotional. Theirs was the dialectic of persuasion rather than of controversy, and for the most part they were content with simply suggesting what later theologians thought it wise to formulate. But their Trinitarianism was none the less emphatic because of its singing and praying itself into expression. When, for example, St. Paul says, "Through Him we both have access, in one Spirit, unto the Father," he is not, to be sure, laying down the dogma of the Trinity as such, but he is using language which perfectly consists with what that dogma teaches, for it is evident that unless we take "access" to God in the superficial sense of admission to heaven as a sort of inclosure, it must mean the being made truly acquainted with heaven's God; and it is equally evident that no one can afford us "access" of this better sort one-half so adequately as a Helper who is able to say of himself: "All things that the Father hath are mine;" "I am the Way;" "He that hath seen Me hath seen the Father."

Similarly we might take scores of New Testament sayings and find in them, not indeed the scholastic phraseology of the dogma of the Trinity, but all that makes the dogma of the Trinity precious to the heart and mind of the believer.

For really the very best account that can be given of the genesis of this dogma is that which traces it to a desire on the part of the early Church to treat Scripture precisely as modern science is treating nature, namely, by the inductive method. Largely viewed, the Old and the New Testaments are the embodiment of a majestic tradition of God. Taken together and as a whole, they make the source of our theology, strictly so called, our knowledge of the nature of the Almighty. It is to them we go when bent on finding out what God is like, when eager to get an answer to Paul's question, Who art thou, Lord? Thus approached, the Scriptures become to the devout explorer of them what the heavens are to the astronomer, or the earth and the sea to the geologist, namely, the storehouse of the data upon which his beliefs are to be built up. The student of science gets together all the facts germane to his inquiry that he can possibly lay hands on, and after a careful comparison of one with another finally settles upon a formula which he deems large enough to correlate and unify them all. This he calls the "law" of the phenomena. It is a loose phrase, but it is the best we have. The dogma of the Trinity is simply the "law of the phenomena," with respect to God's revelation of His nature, as these phenomena present themselves in Holy Scripture; it is the result, that is to say, of applying to the religious annals of a people evidently marked off from all other peoples in a wonderful way the very same method which under the name of "induction" has accomplished in the field of modern chemistry and physics such memorable results. The Old Testament, as we have seen, insists almost passionately upon the truth that God is one; the New, without for a moment disparaging this all-important dogma, does, nevertheless, very significantly intimate that God is three. Now, the mind of the primitive Church meditating upon these things, patiently comparing Scripture with Scripture, and seeking, as far as might be, to reconcile what seemed contrariant utterances of the one oracle, finally found rest in the conclusion that God was to be known and worshipped both as one and three, as one in the sense which excludes dualism, tritheism, and polytheism; as three in the sense which makes it "meet, right, and our bounden duty" to give glory to "Father, Son, and Holy Ghost." The Trinity is grafted upon the unity, not the unity upon the Trinity. There is but one eternal fount of deity. The "Everlasting Kingdom" is monarchical, not triarchical. Yet though the order is eternal which bids us ever name the three in that succession which the Creed observes, none the less are we bound to recognize that equality of nature which lives between every father and every son, since "light from light"* is just as truly light as if it were underived.

It certainly is a most noteworthy fact, however explained, that the lands and races which have become identified with this special doctrine of the divine existence are the lands and races known as "progressive."

As respects the getting at a better knowledge of the universe we inhabit, the heathen mind seems to be absolutely spell-bound. Chinese "science," for example, is the laughing-stock of the Christian peoples; so is Hindoo science; so is Japanese science—although in a sense we ac-

---

* The accurate sense of the "Light of Light" of the Nicene Creed.

count all three of these nationalities civilized, certainly educated. Nor yet has even monotheism pure and simple, the monotheism which exalts singleness, and singleness only, in its doctrine of the being of God, given evidence of its ability so to impregnate the human mind as to make it continually fruitful of new thought. Neither the Hebrew nor the Moslem tradition has associated itself permanently with scientific progress, the inventive achievements of the Saracenic period to the contrary notwithstanding. To monotheism we owe, no doubt, that assured confidence in the oneness of the whole universe of things and forces which is the basis of all modern physics; but it is doubtful whether anything less than a Christian philosophy, with its allowance for diversity and correlation within the very Godhead itself, would have made possible the discoveries which are the jewels in the crown of scientific monism. The age-long problem is the problem of "the many and the one;" and those thinkers are the most likely to make progress in the solving of it whose theological concept has room in it for the thought of manifoldness as well as for the thought of singleness. At least so long as "the kings of modern thought" continue dumb upon this point and have no explanation of their own to offer, it will be open to the maintainers of the Christian faith to attribute to their doctrine of Father, Son, and Holy Ghost that fructifying influence upon human faculty which somehow and from some source or other has in these last days been brought to bear. The very map of the world, with its patches of dark and light, may itself be put in evidence on the Christian side. The areas which the geographers mark "enlightened" are conterminous with Christendom; and by common acknowledgment that which is most central to Christendom is the Creed whose first paragraph begins, "I believe in God the Father;" whose second is freighted with the doctrine of the Son; and whose third opens, "I believe in the Holy Ghost."

Supplementary to the scriptural argument, which from the nature of the case must always be the main dependence of the defenders of Trinitarian dogma, comes the argument from analogy. Our Lord found the natural world and the social world full, both of them, of similitudes singularly helpful to the better understanding of spiritual truth; is there nothing to be gathered from these same regions in illustration of His final and presumably His most significant utterance? Such parables there are, although it must frankly be acknowledged that none of them is absolutely without flaw. But if, as all the commentators are obliged to confess, this same characteristic of partial and limited applicability is found in Christ's own parables, our having to make this admission need not greatly trouble us.

Beginning, then, at the inorganic world, we have the singularly beautiful parable of the sunbeam, all the more significant because of the frequency with which Christ and His apostles appeal to "light" in their expositions of the things of the Spirit. "God is light."

Of the sunbeam we certainly can affirm that it has unity—we say "a beam of light." Yet in the unity of this same sunbeam there coexist these three entities: heat, light, and actinism. No analysis can shake these three completely apart, yet are they three in one as certainly as they are one in three.*

Another striking analogy, also drawn from the inorganic realm, is the parable of the diamond. This similitude is based on what chemists know as the phenomenon of allotropism. There are certain substances—the diamond is one—which, chameleon-like, present themselves in nature under widely different aspects. The three substances known as diamond, graphite, and coal are chemically one and the same element. Burnt in oxygen gas, they yield precisely the same prod-

---

* This analogy was first suggested, so far as the present writer is aware, in a sermon preached many years ago by the Rev. Charles H. Hall, D.D., at that time rector of the Church of the Epiphany, Washington.

uct. In the very deepest and profoundest sense the three are absolutely one, for though each is different, and strikingly different, from the other two, all three are carbon—carbon and nothing else. There is a mystery here undoubtedly, something that eludes and baffles the intelligence; and yet so closely allied is it to the other and heavenly mystery which we are studying that the terms in which the two may be expressed are actually interchangeable. What is meant is that one may take a carefully drawn statement of the dogma of the Trinity, and by writing into it the names of the three allotropic forms of carbon, produce a creed which every chemist will be compelled by the laws of his science to acknowledge as correct, while at the same time confessing that it involves a mystery as real, so far as our present apprehension goes, even if not as intrinsically inexplicable, as the mystery of the Trinity. Even if we take for a standard the severely articulated statements of the Athanasian symbol, the analogy is found to stand the test, for we may say, and say truthfully, diamond is carbon, graphite is carbon, coal is carbon; yet they are not three carbons, but one carbon, though diamond be not graphite, nor graphite coal, nor coal diamond. These material illustrations may possibly grate harshly upon some minds; but when we remember the homely ways in which our Lord Himself deigned to illustrate spiritual verities, we ought not to be startled at finding the diamond and the sunbeam—which have ever been accounted the very synonyms of preciousness—made helpful toward the better understanding of the name of God.

Perhaps, after all, the charge of irreverence lies more justly at the door of those who fail to see the sanctity latent in common things, the awfulness and the mystery of our daily life.

Passing from the inorganic to the psychical world, from the universe of things to the universe of people, some find an analogue of the Trinity in the very constitution of the human soul. This seems a natural thing to do when we recall the memorable sentence, "In the image of God made He man." If the soul does indeed reflect the lineaments of the Maker of the soul, there ought certainly to be discernible on the mirror's face some hint at least of that threefoldness which the Church's dogma attributes to Almighty God.

It is argued that to a complete self-consciousness three elements are essential: first, a self who knows; secondly, a self who is known; and, thirdly, a self who gives assurance that the first self and the second self are one. The last of these constituents of a perfect self-consciousness is lacking in the little child—

"'The baby new to earth and sky,
What time his tender palm is prest
Against the circle of the breast,
Has never thought that 'this is I.'"

He is cognizant, that is to say, of his projected self, but the image is like other images that pass before him; the secret of his personal identity he has yet to learn. Until he has made considerable progress in the art of thinking, he invariably speaks of himself in the third person.*
This is the human analogue of trinity in unity as it shadows itself forth in the case of an individual, and is illustrated by the pure laws of thought. Thus presented, it makes no appeal whatever to the affections. But it is otherwise if we start from that larger conception of man

---

* " Thus the divine personality, in the light thrown upon it by the revealed doctrine of the Trinity, is seen to be wholly independent of the finite. God does not struggle out into self-consciousness by the help of the external universe. Before that universe was created, and in the solitude of His own eternity and self-sufficiency, He had within His own essence all the conditions of self-consciousness. . . . Self-consciousness is trinal, while mere consciousness is dual. The former implies three distinctions; the latter only two. When I am conscious of a tree, there is first a subject, namely, my mind; and secondly an object, namely, the tree. This is all there is in the process of consciousness. But when I am conscious of myself, there is first a subject, namely, my mind as a contemplating mind; there is secondly an object, namely, my mind as a contemplated mind; and thirdly there is still another subject, namely, my mind as perceiving that these two prior distinctions are one and the same mind."—*Sheda's* "*Dogmatic Theology*," vol. 1, p. 189.

which insists that to be truly known he must be studied in his social relations. In the very same sentence in which the author of Genesis affirms that God made man in His own image, it is added "male and female created He them;" while in the clause that follows next after, we further read, "And God said unto them, Be fruitful and multiply."

Thus early is the family, to which are essential the three elements of fatherhood, motherhood, and childhood, recognized as the true completion of man. This analogy, unlike the purely metaphysical one based upon individual self-consciousness, carries us over into the realm of feeling, and imparts a new and deep significance to the saying of St. John the Divine, "God is Love."

A modern author, almost as much theologian as poet, seems to have had this Trinitarian parable in mind when he sketched his picture of a Christian family walking to church—

> "The prudent partner of his blood
> Leaned on him, faithful, gentle, good,
> Wearing the rose of womanhood.
>
> "And in their double love secure,
> The little maiden walked demure,
> Pacing with downward eyelids pure.
>
> "These three made unity so sweet,
> My frozen heart began to beat,
> Remembering its ancient heat."*

---

* "The Two Voices."

Thus much for the analogies by aid of which theologians have sought to interpret to the imagination some of the aspects and significances of the Christian name of God. They are confessedly imperfect and inadequate, as every attempted illustration of the deep things of God must necessarily be, but they are not for that reason wholly without value, and scarcely deserve the contemptuous disregard with which they are sometimes set aside.

It remains to speak briefly of the value of the doctrine of the Trinity as a support and stay to other distinctively Christian beliefs, some of which appear to make a more direct appeal to the hearts and consciences of men than this one itself does. Really this dogma is the keystone of the arch which bridges the chasm between two worlds. All the other doctrines hold their place and keep their steadiness by dint of the stability of this. This is the secret of the position assigned to Trinity Sunday in the scheme of the Christian year. It brings to a head and sums up into one consistent whole all that has been taught from Advent onward to Whitsunday.

Consider, for a single example, the doctrine of the Sacrifice of the death of Christ, than which assuredly no one of the great announcements of Christianity has more profoundly swayed the feelings of mankind.

Take away from this doctrine the support afforded it by the Trinitarian conception of the dignity of the sufferer, and the Cross, from having been the manifestation of a divine self-sacrifice, the pledge and witness of an unconquerable love, becomes instead a terrible suggestion of superhuman cruelty and a most undivine injustice. It is inconceivable that the unrighteous putting to death of an innocent man should have been so acceptable to the divine Majesty as to accomplish the forgiveness of a guilty race. If it was a true Son of God who suffered, we can with some slight measure of clearness discern a reason for the potency of His death. The picture of an angry God looking about for some blameless creature upon whom to pour out the full measure of His wrath never would have converted the world. It has been because He was recognized as more and other than a creature that the Christ of history has shown men with such marvellous effect "His hands and His side." It has been by a sequence strictly logical that the rejection of the sacrificial element in Christian theology has always followed so swiftly upon the relinquishment of the Trinitarian ground.

I trust I have said enough to show that the end and purpose of the dogma of a divine trinity in unity is to help rather than to baffle the mind of the believer in it. It is an endeavor after doctrinal harmony, an end not wholly attainable so long as the human intellect is curtained as it is, and yet an end which none need feel ashamed of having aimed at. For even ineffectual strivings after a better apprehension of spiritual truth have their value, and it is good to ponder the things eternal, even though our estimations of them fall short of the full weight. I would rather "know in part" the mountain than know perfectly the mole-hill.

Do you assure me that it would be far wiser to devote a like amount of energy to the promotion of practical religion? Practical religion! Ah, how we cheat ourselves with phrases! Show me the man whose soul is full of heavenly imaginings, who dwells largely among things not seen, whose thoughts often take flight from the edges of this buying and selling world, that they may strike out into the pure air and find rest upon the wing as the sea-birds do, and I will show you one who will make the best of neighbors, the most public-spirited of citizens, the gentlest, kindest, truest, least arrogant of men. For, after all, the great thing in "practical religion" is to sink self, and in this task we succeed best at moments when most we realize the littleness of man, the majesty of the Almighty. Therefore with angels and archangels, and with all the company of heaven, we laud and magnify thy glorious Name; evermore praising Thee and saying,
"Holy, Holy, Holy!"

The Incarnation.

THE REV. ALFRED G. MORTIMER, D.D.,

Rector of S. Mark's Church, Philadelphia.

The Incarnation.

As we scan the fields of the Church's history from its earliest days till now, the names of three Apostles rise up before us, representing with more or less accuracy the three types of thought which have engrossed the mind and colored the view of the Christian world: S. Peter, S. Paul, and S. John.

S. Peter, associated with the idea of church organization and government, naturally comes first in the order of time; since the first work was necessarily the spread and development of the Church—for of Christianity as dissociated from the Church, as some would teach it now, I fail to discover the faintest sign in antiquity.

This idea is the most prominent for fifteen centuries, often unduly pressed and unwarrantably developed and unjustly claiming the shelter of S. Peter's name for much that he would have been the first to repudiate.

In the sixteenth century we see a great revolution in the thought and life of the Church, which we are accustomed to speak of as the Reformation, and which claimed as its authority the teachings of S. Paul. From church polity the minds of men were turned to Soteriology, to the great doctrine of the Atonement and the results which were thought to flow from it; and again, as in S. Peter's case, much was deduced from S. Paul's words at which he would himself probably have stood aghast.

Our lives are cast in the beginning of a third period, which, when its history comes to be written, will, I think, be found to have been as great a revolution in religious life and thought as the Reformation was, though I hope and believe less marred by human passion and sin, more truly a period of progress and peace.

And this third period looks for its guidance chiefly to the writings of S. John.

We are beset to-day with perplexities, not new, and perhaps not greater than in the past, but presenting themselves under new aspects, and, from the increased facilities of communication which the press affords, forced upon our notice with a vehemence and persistence from which there is no escape. Questions crave an answer, problems demand a solution, and we are beginning to find the answer in the fuller realization, the clearer grasp of the doctrine of the Incarnation. We are learning that *that* is the centre of all revelation, of all truth, and that many of our difficulties, both theological and practical, are the results of the failure to recognize the true position and significance of the Incarnation, or of an attempt to substitute for it some other centre around which to harmonize Christian truth.

As we look back on the difficulties which beset astronomers before the sixteenth century, from the acceptance of the Ptolemaic theory, and their attempt to bring all things into relation with the earth as the centre of the solar system, and observe how most of them disappeared as soon as the true centre of our planetary system was recognized; so we see how for many years the theology of our Church has been made to centre around the doctrine of the Atonement, which is not the true centre, but itself the necessary sequence of the Incarnation in its relation to sin. And the discovery, if I may so speak, of the Incarnation as the true centre, has swept away many of the greatest difficulties of theology, and promises, as we grasp it more fully and realize its consequence more clearly, to be the solution of much that is perplexing us now in social as well as in theological problems.

Our difficulties arising from a false view of the Atonement have led to wrong and perverted views both of God and man. And the popular Protestantism of the day invites the attack of unbelievers, who naturally score an easy victory over what is itself a perversion and distortion of the truth.

The Incarnation is to us the great revelation of God; for in Christ "dwelleth all the fulness of the Godhead bodily-wise." (Col. ii. 9.) But the

Incarnation is also the great revelation of man, of his strength, of his possibilities of good, man as God made him, and meant him to be; for in *fallen* man we have to study human nature marred and distorted by sin, which is an element foreign to man as God purposed him to be. Now in studying any intricate piece of mechanism, it is an immense help at the start if we know the purpose for which it was made.

The Incarnation is the revelation of the purpose for which man was created, the goal for which he must aim, the perfection to which he must attain. And in a clearer comprehension of man himself, the heart-searching problems of man's relation to his fellow man, in capital and labor, in poverty and riches, in politics and society, find their only true solution.

The theology of the Incarnation then must be the theology of our Era, and to its study we may turn, not merely as to an intellectual exercise of great interest, but as to a revelation of life of immense practical and present value.

What then is this doctrine of the Incarnation? In its most concise statement it is contained in the proposition of S. John, "The Word was made Flesh," and the whole of his Epistles and Gospel are but an amplification of this text.

In order to understand what took place at the Incarnation, we must first strive to grasp the relation in which God stood to the world and to man before that event; in a word, we must know something of the Gospel of Creation, for without a clear view of this, we are likely in many important points to misread the Gospel of Redemption.

Briefly, we may put the opinion of theologians on this matter somewhat as follows: When God in His infinite love willed to create, He created all things for a perfect end; for this His attribute of Omnipotence demands, but this ultimate perfection was to be attained by a law of progress, the stages of which may be read in the Annals of the Universe. Confining ourselves as we must to our planet, we may perhaps, for convenience' sake, group the stages of this progress into four great epochs or chapters. I. The development of inorganic matter till it is fitted to receive and sustain organic life. II. The development of this organic life until man appears. III. Commencing with man, the unfolding and growth of moral life until culminating in the Incarnation. IV. The introduction and operation of the Divine life.

It has been said that all Creation is a ladder by which we may climb up into the heart of God, and see there His love for us, and this is also true when regarded from a different point of view. For that Creation which comes forth from God by the fiat of His will progresses step by step, until in the Incarnation it returns to Him again.

For as each act of creation was on God's part an act of voluntary self-limitation, and the climax of that self-limitation was reached in the Incarnation, when God the Word emptied Himself, and took upon Him the form of servant; so after the Atonement had been made and mankind (and in man all creatures) had been redeemed by the glorification and exaltation of Christ's Humanity, the self-limitation is effaced again, and God becomes all in all. In God's original purpose, or, as S. John Damascene calls it, His antecedent Will, God willed everything to march steadily forward step by step to perfection, the material universe finding its crown and flower, its true representative, in Man, who, created in the image of God (and intended by his own progress to gain the likeness of God), was to be the instrument of God's supreme act of love in the Incarnation. Man by his body summing up all the lower kingdoms of Creation, by the spirit, which he shared with the angelic natures, linked to God, and through the operation of the Holy Spirit holding close communion with God; and when man had reached a certain perfection here, the climax of God's purpose would have been the Incarnation, which, without suffering or humiliation, would have been the taking of man, and in him all creation, into God, not by any pantheistic idea of absorption, but by the fulfilment of God's original purpose, by which the creature should attain its ultimate perfection in Christ, to the glory of God and to its own immense and final beatitude. This would have made the Incarnation the last act in the great drama, the addition of the capping stone to the great structure, the realization of the great Ideal; for in the Word, God saw all creation ideally perfect.

We read the history of the earlier chapters in the science of geology, the record of the marvellous progress of our globe. We see the development of the creature through the various kingdoms of mineral, vegetable and animal life, culminating in Man, in whom we see a new departure, the introduction of a conscious moral life; and that progress would have gone on in the wonderful development of moral life, so far as we know, but for two catastrophes, two interruptions which led to some modifications, if one may use the term, of the original march of progress.

These two interruptions were the Fall of the Angels and the Fall of Man, the introduction of sin (which means philologically " missing the mark "), and which results necessarily in confusion, disorder, and the loss of that communion with God which our first parents had.

For while in one sense the whole creation was outside of God before the Incarnation, which was therefore as necessary for the angels as for Man,

THE INCARNATION.

yet when God created Man in His own image, a very close communion between God and Man existed through the operation of the Holy Spirit; this was what was lost by the Fall, and besides, disorder and confusion took the place of harmony and peace.

While this was no part of God's original purpose or Antecedent Will, it was present as a possibility to God's foreknowledge, and was provided for by His Consequent Will. For when He willed to create moral beings with a power of choice, that they might love God and choose good, there was of necessity the possibility of evil. Without this power of choice, without this possibility of evil, we might do good, but we could not love good; we might be excellent machines, we could not be moral agents.

So we are told that before the Fall, in the time of man's innocency, there were in the Garden of Eden two trees—the tree of life and the tree of the knowledge of good and evil; the tree of life representing the fellowship and communion with God which was to be at once man's joy and the means of his progress; the tree of knowledge representing that knowledge of evil which is necessary, that we may deliberately honor God by choosing good, by choosing Him. Evil must be present, as a thing known and contemplated, as God knows and contemplates it only to hate it, never to experience it. Adam was not satisfied thus to contemplate it and to hate it, but wished to taste it, to experience it. In a word, by his deliberate act he chose it and he fell, and in the experience of evil he lost the fruit of that other tree, the tree of life, the power of communion with God. His nature lost its sustaining power and collapsed; there was not the introduction of anything new in human nature, but there was the withdrawal of the fellowship with God, the loss of the continual operation of the Spirit, and the introduction of disorder and struggle between the various powers of his nature which before had been harmoniously balanced.

From the Fall a new preparation for the Incarnation became necessary, and began in the training and development of the human race for this end. First in the selection of one particular race trained by type, prophecy, theophany, and legislation, to be the instrument for the accomplishment of God's loving purpose. But our view would be very partial if we limited this preparation to Judaism. Everywhere it was going on, in the natural theology as well as in the art and science, the literature and civilization of the various races of the world. For as S. John says, the Word was "the Light that lighteth every man that cometh into the World," and the Eastern mystics, the poets of the Vedas, the astronomers of Chaldea, and the priests of Egypt alike were learning, though with difficulty, to spell out God's revelation in nature. Greek Philosophy and Art and Literature, Roman Polity and Commerce alike were being prepared by God's Providence for the revelation of the Incarnate Word.

The Greeks were not only to supply the most perfect language the world has ever known to enshrine His revelation, but also to train men's minds to receive and apply it; for we must bear in mind that the great fathers of the Church, such as Clement and Origen, Athanasius and Augustine, Gregory and Basil, were thoroughly familiar with Greek philosophy, and testify what it had done for their souls in preparing them to receive, and afterward to teach the religion of the Incarnation. Even those splendid Roman roads, which are still memorials of the energy and thoroughness of that great nation, and along which its Commerce went forth through the World, even they themselves are the literal fulfilment of the prophecy of Isaiah xl. 3, " Prepare ye the way of the Lord, make straight in the desert a *highway* for our God"; for they were trodden by the feet of Apostles and Missionaries bearing the Gospel of the Incarnation to the ends of the Earth. The very difficulty which has been suggested by some sceptics, that there are parallelisms and resemblances between the moral precepts of some earlier religions and the Sermon on the Mount, though the former are but faint shadows of that great reality, so far from being difficulties to the believer in the Incarnation, are but proofs of the truth of S. Paul's words, that among all nations "the living God left not Himself without witness." While those adumbrations of Christian doctrine, practice, and ritual, which may be traced with more or less distinctness in almost every ancient system of religion, are the very things to which the theologian of the Incarnation points as the proof that all human nature was being trained to receive the Gospel of the Incarnation, that the Word was indeed the Light of the World. Socrates and Heraclitus with all enlightened heathen, Justin Martyr, the first apologist, claims as practically Christians, because illuminated by the true light; and may we not add to the list Plato? Recall that splendid passage in his Phoedrus, where he describes the gods in solemn procession mounting to the topmost vault of heaven and taking their places upon its dome, gazing over the infinite depths of perfect Truth, and finding in the spectacle the support of the fulness of their being; and again in the Republic, that marvellous passage where he declares the fate of the perfectly righteous man in this world, and says that he will be "scourged, racked, fettered, will have his eyes burnt out, and at last, after suffering every kind of torture, will be crucified."

Yes, we recognize and claim every advance towards truth in all lands, even where mingled with error, as the work of the Divine Word in the World, co-operating with human reason, inspiring some like the Jews with a thirst for holiness, others like the Greeks with intellectual eagerness after truth, and preparing all for the revelation of the Incarnation.

But after the Fall of man, instead of the Incarnation being, as it would have been but for sin, the final step in a perfected Humanity, by which Man was translated, so to speak, into heaven itself, and in him Creation returned into God, from Whom it had come forth, and Who in His love had originally called it into being. Instead of the Incarnation being the last act in the Gospel of Creation, it came as the foundation of a further Gospel of Redemption, rendered necessary by the fact that from sin the moral progress of Humanity had practically come to a standstill, and the bitter experience of the race had brought home to human consciousness that it was powerless to help itself, and that without God's intervention and aid, it could advance no further towards the goal of perfection. The Incarnation then became—in addition to its original purpose of taking man and in him all Creation into God,—also the means by which what was lost through the Fall was to be restored. Divine Life was introduced to aid the weakened moral life of man, and the arrested progress recommenced, though still fettered by the results of sin. And from this by necessary sequence the Atonement followed, a superinduced result of a cause not originally present, viz.: Sin.

But what was the Incarnation as a fact? The taking of Man into God, not by a fusion of the Human and Divine natures, but, while each nature was kept perfectly distinct, by the uniting of both in the Person of the Word, the Eternal Son of God, the Second Person of the ever Blessed Trinity. The means was the operation of the Holy Ghost upon the substance of the Blessed Virgin Mary, by which act the Word became the Son of Man, without being the Son of *a* man; and so took into Himself Humanity without taking Adam's taint of original sin. This Virgin-birth is not only an Article of Faith in the Church, but it also commends itself to our reason as the only way, so far as we can see, by which the purpose of the Incarnation could be accomplished, and Humanity taken into God without taking also sin. And let me observe in passing that, so far from the doctrine of Parthenogenesis being contrary to reason, it is not even contrary to experience; instances of both entire and partial parthenogenesis are found in many species in nature, the most familiar being that of the queen bee and the drones. It is, I say, so far as we can see, the only way in which the problem could be solved, whereby a new Head of Humanity should be produced in such a manner that, while the *moral* entail of descent from Adam should be broken and thus the taint of sin avoided, yet the connection with Adam should remain intact through the female line, in all that appertained to the essentials of Humanity; the fecundating power being supplied directly by the Lord and Life-giver, the Holy Ghost.

And so the Creed tells us that our Lord was made "*Man*," not "*a* man." It was Manhood, not a man (although He may be spoken of as a man), human nature, not a human person, that the Son of God took into union with Himself, and it is of the utmost importance to any clear understanding of the Incarnation to grasp this.

By human nature we mean all those qualities which men have in common; by a human person we mean a separate individual, possessing that individual and sovereign power of action in the soul to which we give the name of personality.

Now Adam did not transmit to his descendants his personality, for that is incommunicable, but his nature. No human being can part with his own personality or share it with another.

When Adam begat sons and daughters he passed on to his offspring his own nature in its fulness, but his personality remained exclusively his own forever, and his descendants had each their own personality. Personality then is no essential part of human nature, but human nature is organized on a new personality in every individual, and therefore it is not so difficult to understand, that in order to cut off the entail of that tainted *moral* nature which we derive from Adam, and in order to make the Hypostatic Union of the Divine and Human natures possible, the germ of Humanity which was derived from Adam through the Blessed Virgin, was vitalized by the direct operation of the Holy Ghost, the Lord and Lifegiver, and instead of being, like ours, centred in a new human personality, was taken up into the Personality of the Word. So that all that was essential to Humanity was taken up by the Second Adam, and the differences between our Lord's Humanity and ours, that He had no human father, no human person, and no sin, are none of them differences which touch in any way the integrity and perfection of His Human Nature.

Around the fact of the Incarnation in the early ages of the Church four false propositions arose, and took shape as definite heresies, which were condemned after thorough examination by the first four General Councils; the opposite truth in each case being defined authoritatively by the Church.

First there was the Arian heresy, which, denying the truth that Christ was really God, attacked the perfection of His Divine Nature. This, as you are aware, was refuted by the Council of Nicea, A.D. 325, which defined His Divine Nature in the Creed which we recite, by the use of the word Homo-ousios, "of the same substance" as the Father.

Then came a reaction, and Apollinarius, while accepting the Nicene decree as to the Divine Nature of our Lord, denied the reality and perfection of His Humanity, by asserting that He had no human soul or "*nous*," the place thereof being supplied by the person of the Word. Now this was taking away from the integrity of our Lord's Human Nature, since a human or rational soul is an essential part of humanity, and indeed is that which differentiates man alike from the angels and the beasts. This heresy was condemned by the Second General Council, that of Constantinople, A.D. 381.

Then arose the heresy of Nestorius, who, while accepting the decrees of Nicea and Constantinople as to the perfection of the two natures of our Lord, taught that He had also two personalities, a human personality as well as a Divine personality, thus denying any real union between God and Man in the Incarnation. This was condemned by the Third General Council, that of Ephesus, A.D. 431. And as a reaction from this, Eutyches taught that as there was but one Person, so there was but one Nature in our Lord, and that this was a sort of fusion of the Human and Divine in the formation of a third composite nature. This heresy was condemned by the Fourth General Council, that of Chalcedon, A.D. 451.

Hence we have in our Lord two perfect natures, Human and Divine, distinct and yet united hypostatically in one Divine Personality in the Person of Our Lord.

When we have reached this definition of the Hypostatic Union, a further question arises, which is one of the problems to which the minds of theologians are being especially directed in our own time, and that is, as to the accommodation of these two natures to one another, so as to make this Hypostasis or Incarnation possible; what did it involve to the Divine Nature, to God the Son? We can easily comprehend that as Humanity was created in the image of God, it might be ultimately taken into God; in a word, that as it was created for the Incarnation, it would easily accommodate itself to the Divine Nature; but the difficulty is to grasp the fact that the Divine shrunk itself, as it were, to the conditions of the inferior nature which it assumed. This, like every other aspect of the Incarnation, we find set forth in the Old Testament in type, as for instance in I. Kings xvii. 21, where we read that Elijah stretched (or measured) himself three times on the dead child of the widow of Zarephath, and still more strikingly, in II. Kings iv. 34, where Elisha, so to speak, accommodated and contracted himself to the small form of the son of the Shunamite, putting "his mouth upon his mouth, and his eyes upon his eyes, and his hands upon his hands." The little light which Scripture throws on this mysterious subject comes from three passages, Phil. ii. 6, 7: "Who, being in the form of God, thought it not a prize to be snatched at to be equal with God, but emptied Himself, and took upon Himself the form of a servant." The second, II. Cor. viii. 9: "Who being rich, for our sakes became poor," and the third, S. John xvii. 5: "And now, O Father, glorify Thou me with Thine own Self with the glory which I had with Thee before the world was." From the expression used by S. Paul in the first of these passages, "He emptied Himself," the subject is commonly spoken of as the Kenosis of our Lord, His Self-emptying. The question is a very difficult one, and we are helped neither by the discussions of Councils, nor by the writings of the Fathers, who with most theologians till our day contented themselves with making the Kenosis consist in the laying aside the Glory of the Divinity, and in the assumption of the humiliation of the Humanity; but while this is undoubtedly true, some theologians of the present day feel it to be very inadequate, and are asking for a more complete investigation of the question. The most familiar theories are those of Gess, Martensen, Thomasius, Ebrard and Pabst, representing almost every shade of opinion, Pabst being a Roman Catholic; and it is easier to criticise these theories, and show where they are untenable, and even heretical, than it is to construct one which shall answer all the conditions of the question.

Some would say, why discuss at all a question so mysterious? Would it not be wiser and more reverent to pass it over, as so many theologians have done? Is it a matter of any practical value to Christianity to-day? My answer is, Yes; that is the only reason why it must be faced; for if we believe that the Incarnation contains in itself the answer to many of the perplexities of human life to-day, we must teach the perfect Humanity of our Lord without surrendering His perfect Divinity on the one hand, or on the other allowing our conception of that Divinity so to overshadow His Human life as to make it unreal. It is the neglect of this which is leading the Rationalistic School in our Church to-day in their Humanitarianism to drift so perilously near to Arianism, as a reaction from that obscuration of the perfect Humanity by a view of the Divinity, which, because it overlooks the Kenosis, robs the work of our Lord of much of its power to appeal to our sympathy and to help us in our needs, because it seems to rob His Human life of its reality.

And while most of us realize the terrible dangers which threaten us from Rationalistic Christianity, many of us do not see that it gains strength from our not putting forth in all its completeness the doctrine of the Incarnation, as defined by the first four General Councils; and some who pride themselves on their ultra orthodoxy, in their fear of Rationalism, by ignoring our Lord's Kenosis, are practically teaching a subtle form of either Eutychianism or Nestorianism. For there are two views which are open to criticism as tending to these two heresies, and which are held by some even of those who think that Arianism is the danger of the day.

There is that view which, by attributing Divine Omniscience to the human intelligence of the Child Jesus, is dangerously near to such a confusion of the natures as approaches the Eutychian error and practically results in the loss of the Human in the Divine. While others, in avoiding this, and dwelling upon the natural human ignorance of the Child of Mary, imply that He was not yet really the Word Himself, but only joined to the Word in such a way as to allow the Word Himself to live on outside of the human being to which He was joined; on the one hand suggesting a double personality, which is distinctly Nestorian, and on the other reducing the earthly life of Jesus to a mere Docetic illusion, which satisfies neither the cravings of our nature for a Divine Saviour, nor the definitions of the Church as to the Incarnation.

Most of those who are brought into real contact with the theological controversies of the day will, I think, recognize these dangers, and feel that to meet them we must teach, in all its completeness, the Faith as defined by the General Councils: and that we cannot do this, in connection with the thought of to-day, without recognizing, as a real fact, that Kenosis of the Divine Word which S. Paul teaches, and which is implicitly contained in the authoritative condemnation of the heresies of the fourth and fifth centuries. At the end of a lecture like this, I can do no more than try to state some of the conditions of the problem, first reminding you of the impossibility of grasping with our finite minds any Divine truth in all its eternal fulness, much less that truth which S. Paul calls "the great mystery of Godliness, God manifested in the flesh," and the further impossibility of finding human language adequate to the expression of Divine truth of such transcendent magnitude. We who live in *time* are not capable of grasping the relations between time and eternity; so that the practical treatment of the Kenosis must be confined to an investigation of the conditions of our Lord's real life on earth, without dogmatizing on what that involved to His eternal life in the bosom of the Father; only insisting that when the Creed tells us that "He came down from Heaven," we mean that there was a real coming down, and not merely that, to an unchangeable Divine consciousness, another human consciousness was added, but that there was a real emptying of Himself of something He possessed. It is almost superfluous to observe that, as S. Paul points out, the change involved in this Kenosis is a change in form, not in essence, and that while on the one hand a limitation of the attributes is demanded, yet it was a voluntary self-limitation, and all the time that those Divine powers were quiescent within Him, they were still His, and had He chosen to revoke this self-restraint, there was nothing outside of His own will to hinder Him. Yet while acknowledging this voluntary self-limitation of Christ, we must preserve in thought His relation both to the essential life of the Holy Trinity, and to the universe of which He is the continual support, whose unity and order He continually maintains.

So we acknowledge and adore, from the first moment of His Conception, the Child of Mary as perfectly Divine, all the fulness of the Godhead dwelling in Him bodily-wise, and yet as fulfilling all the conditions of His gradually unfolding Human life. We see Him hungry and thirsty and weary, tempted, suffering, dying, dead! "Perfect God and perfect Man; of a reasonable soul and human flesh subsisting. Who, although He be God and Man; yet He is not two, but one Christ!" So far the doctrine of the Incarnation. One word in conclusion as to its practical bearing on the difficulties and problems of to-day.

The theology of the Incarnation hails as a friend, not as an enemy, the man of science patiently striving to wrest from nature some of her secrets, and she gratefully adds to the sum total of truth his contribution, however small. While lamenting his personal loss in his own inability to see Divine truth, she delights to trace all the discoveries of science to that Light which lighteth every man, to that Providence which educates the world for the ultimate triumph of Christ! The theology of the Incarnation takes the lover of Art by the hand and leads him through the galleries of Europe, where he sees how Art, as the handmaid of the Word made Flesh, grew and developed from its first crude efforts on the walls of the Catacombs, in Cloister and Church, till in the Vatican she bids him stand before its highest conception, in the Transfiguration of Raphael, and Domenichino's Last Communion of S. Jerome, and points out to him that it was not by portraying the realistic or rather materialistic side of nature in such a way as to appeal to the baser passions of man's sensuality, not by descending to the mere depicting of man in his sin, but by representing the highest ideals of Humanity which gather around the religion of the Incarnation, that Art learned its powers and found its goal!

The theology of the Incarnation points the masses who are struggling with poverty, misery and sin, to its Founder, Who, though He was rich, for our sakes became poor, that we, through His poverty, might be rich; Who gave, when challenged at a critical moment of His career, as the distinguishing mark of the truth of His mission, this law, "To the poor the Gospel is preached."

The theology of the Incarnation approaches the laborer in his contests with capital, in his hardships and toils, as the religion of the Carpenter's Son Who ennobled work and taught men to labor and to wait!

To the people groaning under the wrongs and injustice of political tyranny, it comes and shows One Who gathered around Him poor fishermen, and taught them the principles which have since emancipated the world!

To the Social Reformer burning with indignation at the degradation of morals, it comes with the example of Him Who, to lift man from his misery and sin, laid down His life alike for friend and foe.

There is not one phase of human progress, not one step forward towards Goodness, Beauty, or Truth, of which the theology of the Incarnation does not claim that Christ is the Inspiration and the Incarnation the Beacon Light!

The Atonement.

LECTURE IV.
THE ATONEMENT.

BY

REV. JOHN H. ELLIOTT, S.T.D.,

Rector of the Church of the Ascension, Washington, D.C.

IN the tenth book of "the City of God," St. Augustine quotes from a philosopher the complaint that "there was wanting some universal method of delivering men's souls, which no sect of philosophers had ever yet found out." St. Augustine replies that the universal method of delivering men's souls, which no philosopher had found out, had been taught by Divine authority. Divine authority had taught that the "Lord Jesus took our manhood upon Himself, and in that manhood took this priesthood upon Himself, and sacrificed Himself even to the death for us. This," says he, "is the universal way of the soul's freedom, that is granted unto all nations out of God's mercy, the knowledge whereof comes and is to come to all men."

"The knowledge whereof is to come to all men." It has come to us. On a continent un known to the great Latin Father—in a "city" of which he had no prophetic vision, we have assembled to think about "the universal method of freeing men's souls" by the atonement of our Lord and Saviour Jesus Christ. We too have felt the need of the soul's deliverance from the burden and bondage of sin. We have not found "deliverance" in any school of philosophy. Like St. Augustine, we yield to the Divine authority, and trust those "divinely guided prophets and apostles," whom he calls, "holy immortals in religion." We have received across the centuries the faith once for all delivered to the saints. We cherish as the charter of our spiritual emancipation the Catholic dogma of the atonement.

If my first duty in discussing the Catholic dogma of the atonement is to ask what is dogma? I shall answer that question in the words of one of the great advocates and exponents of dogma. "Dogma," says the late Canon Liddon, "is essential Christian truth thrown by authority into a form which admits of its permanently passing into the understanding, and being treasured by the heart of the people. Dogma proclaims that Revelation does mean something and what. Accordingly, dogma is to be found no less truly in the volume of the New Testament than in Fathers and Councils. The Divine Spirit, speaking through the clear utterances of Scripture and the illuminated and consenting thought of Christendom, is the real author of essential dogma. And men of to-day who are calling in question the principles of dogma are calling in question a central inalienable feature of Christianity which has been always accepted alike by Rome and Lambeth and Lambeth and Geneva, as a common premise, as an axiomatic principle." *

But your subject this evening is the "Catholic Dogma of the Atonement;" and so another preliminary question is, Where shall you and I look for and find "Catholic dogma?" I trust that you will agree with me when I say that, as loyal churchmen, we look for and find Catholic dogma in that volume which, in its completeness, I shall call the Book of Common Prayer. Our Book of Common Prayer was designed to be also our Book of Common *Faith* and Common *Doctrine*. Surely we believe that no Catholic dogma has been excluded from its pages, that no un-Catholic dogma has been suffered to intrude there.

In that Book dogma abounds—abounds in Creed and Collect, in triumphant Te Deum and lowliest litany. "There," to repeat the words of Canon Liddon, you find " essential Christian truth thrown by authority into a form which admits of its permanently passing into the understanding and being treasured by the heart of the people."

---
* Liddon's " University Sermons " (Sermon Fourth).

It is indeed dogma, "essential Christian truth," which chiefly in that Book interests the understanding and gains the hearts of the people. It is because of dogma in its pages that there throb there "the profound emotion, the grave eloquence, the noble mindedness, the restrained enthusiasm of heroic and poetic souls." And an oft-quoted canon subscribed by the Bishops of both Provinces in the Church of England A.D. 1571, seems to give the sanction of their authority to the statement that we are to look to the Book of Common Prayer for Catholic dogma. The canon enjoins upon "preachers that they shall in the first place be careful never to teach anything from the pulpit, to be religiously held and believed by the people, but what is agreeable to the doctrine of the Old or New Testament, and collected out of that very doctrine by the *Catholic* Fathers and Ancient Bishops; and since these articles of the Christian religion, which have been agreed upon by the Bishops in a lawful and holy synod, are beyond doubt, collected out of the sacred books of the Old and New Testaments, and agree in all things with the heavenly doctrine contained in them, and since the Book of Public Prayers, and the Book of the Consecration of Bishops, Priests, and Deacons contain nothing opposed to that doctrine, whoever are sent to teach the people shall confirm the authority and truth of those articles."* Does not the canon seem to imply that the rule here laid down for the pulpit is the rule which had been followed in the Book of Common Prayer? Does it not seem to teach that for dogma in the pulpit and for dogma in the Book of Common Prayer there was one rule: "It must be agreeable to the doctrine of the Old or New Testament, and collected out of that very doctrine by the *Catholic* Fathers and Ancient Bishops?"

Turning then to no new guide but to the familiar Book of Common Prayer, which we love so well, we find there a doctrine of the atonement of which we may say: *First*, that it is "an harmonious balance of complementary truths." *Secondly*, that, founded on Divine authority, it accepts mystery instead of banishing mystery by human system. *Thirdly*, that it pays due and consistent honor to Holy Scripture; and, *Fourthly*, that its fulness satisfies the desire for an "universal method of freeing men's souls."

I. In the first place the Catholic dogma of the atonement, as enshrined in the Book of Common Prayer, is an "harmonious balance of complementary truths—of truths which," in the words of Canon Mozley, "have the point of view which brings them all together in the invisible world." On authority it presents to faith truths as com-

---
* Sparrow's "Collection."

plementary which are often treated as contradictory one of another. It includes the love and *mercy* of God the Father in giving His Only Son to suffer death on the Cross for our redemption, and yet the *satisfaction* for the sins of the world which the Son made there by His one oblation of Himself, once offered. It includes in their integrity the truth and value of the Incarnation, that the sufferings of Christ were the "sufferings of One in whom we live and who lives in us," and yet the substitution of Christ as the "very Paschal Lamb which was offered for us and hath taken away the sin of the world." It includes in the atonement a ransom *for* the souls of men, and yet a moral and mystical influence *on* the souls of men. It gives full, hearty recognition to each one of these complementary truths. It does not select one, and by a logic here misapplied press it to the exclusion of the complementary truth which rests on the same authority. Nor does it presume to make a logical adjustment of the complementary truths, and thus mutilate and impoverish them. Why impoverish by statement of finite logic what Hooker calls "the Infinite worth of the Son of God?" Why narrow the Divine breadth of God's wisdom in redemption? Is it not like Him that His thoughts should not be as our thoughts?

1. Let me select from the several pairs of com-

plementary truths just stated the first pair, that I may contrast the partial statements made by some leaders or schools or epochs in theology with the Catholic teaching of the Book of Common Prayer. In the Prayer of Consecration, in the order for the administration of the Holy Communion are these words: "All Glory be to Thee Almighty God, our Heavenly Father, for that Thou of Thy tender mercy didst give Thine Only Son Jesus Christ to suffer death upon the Cross for our Redemption, who made there by His one oblation of Himself once offered a full, perfect, and sufficient sacrifice oblation and satisfaction for the sins of the whole world." Here we celebrate on the one hand the *mercy* of the Father in giving His Only Son, and yet on the other hand the *satisfaction* made by the Son in His willing oblation of Himself. The blending of these truths in one statement is the more significant, when we remember to whom the satisfaction on the Cross was made. " The death of the Lord Jesus paid the debt which man owed and which man of himself could not pay to the Justice and Sanctity of God. His obedience to the Divine will took the form of expiation, and became a satisfaction for sin to the All-Just."[*] And yet, in our communion office, each truth is recognized and enshrined in its integrity, in Divine

---
[*] Canon Liddon.

fulness—in absolute completeness. We speak of the mercy of Almighty God, our Heavenly Father, in the gift of His Son, of His tender mercy. We praise Him for His mercy: "All glory be to Thee Almighty God, our Heavenly Father, for that Thou of Thy tender mercy didst give Thine Only Son." In like absolute completeness the satisfaction made on the Cross is stated: "Who made there by His one oblation of Himself, once offered, a full, perfect, and sufficient . . . satisfaction for the sins of the world "—" full, perfect, sufficient," as against all limitations of the atonement. Side by side in one sentence are presented the complementary truths—the tender mercy of the Father and the satisfaction made by the Son.

How different from this the partial statements often advocated by leaders, or schools, or epochs in theology! These two truths are treated as exclusive one of another—as contradictory, not complementary. At one time the "satisfaction" is accepted as the great revealed verity, and a logic too presumptuous in its dealings with things revealed would argue out of existence the tender mercy of the Heavenly Father. At another time the "tender mercy" is accepted as the great revealed verity, and the same too presumptuous logic insists that there is no need of "satisfaction." Doubtless, in these later centuries and until this present generation, the doctrine of the satisfaction of Christ has been too exclusively presented. I do not mean that the worth or the completeness of the satisfaction has been exaggerated. It is "full, perfect, sufficient" for the sins of the whole world. But the satisfaction made and the law satisfied have been used as a premise for obscuring the tender mercy and the love of our Heavenly Father. Popular and unskilful advocates of that perfect redemption and satisfaction—rationalists dishonoring Revelation, though they knew it not—have represented the Heavenly Father as granting pardon passively or even reluctantly in view of the legal demands of the "agony and bloody sweat." Learned advocates, too, holding high and honored places in schools of instruction, give definitions of the atonement which contain no hint that God so "loved the world as to give His Only-Begotten Son" for our redemption. Listen to the following definition by an honored Professor in this city: "The atonement is the satisfaction of Divine Justice for the sin of man by the substituted penal sufferings of the Son of God." True, the same teacher elsewhere says: "The mercy of God consists in substituting Himself Incarnate for His creature for purposes of atonement." But the definition of the atonement, formally and pointedly introducing a hundred pages of the history of the doctrine of the atonement—even if it correctly states the doctrine of satisfaction—absolutely omits all reference to the love and mercy of the Heavenly Father.

What wonder that there has been a recoil and reaction; and who can wonder, with the history of human speculation on Divine Mysteries before him, that the mistakes which had been made on the one side are being repeated on the other? Let us be thankful, indeed, for the recognition and assertion of the tender mercy of our Heavenly Father in the atonement. But we would be more thankful to the many noble souls, whose mission it may have been to rescue from partial obscuration this truth, if in their advocacy they would avoid the mistakes which made a rescue of this truth necessary. The advocates of the satisfaction of Christ obscured the mercy of God; the advocates of the tender mercy of the Heavenly Father obscure the satisfaction of Christ. Sometimes they do more than obscure it. More grateful would we be to them if, still, holding with Bishop Butler, that "God hath *mercifully provided* that there should be an interposition to prevent the destruction of human kind," they would also hold with Bishop Butler the "satisfaction" of Christ. Indeed, they would the more celebrate the tender mercy of God, if in the same rejoicing accents they celebrate the satisfaction on the

Cross. That has befallen the exclusive advocates of either of these two truths which usually befals those who undertake to improve on the Revelation of God. They despoil the favorite truth which they would enrich. The satisfaction of Christ the more magnifies the law and makes it honorable when it magnifies the Love that sought to save but would not save with dishonor to the law—and for the tender mercy of God—the love of God—the Apostle declares that *Herein is love*— that God loved us and gave His Son to be a *propitiation* for our sins. It is because our Eucharistic office enshrines both these truths, and thus magnifies each that it summons us to such profound and grateful adoration.

2. In like manner the Catholic doctrine of the atonement includes the second pair of complementary truths above mentioned. It includes both the *substitution* of Christ—that " He was the very Paschal Lamb which was offered for us," and also the Incarnation of the Son of God, that " He took to Himself not some one person among men, but the nature that is common to all," so that His sufferings " were the sufferings of *One in whom we live and who lives in us.*" May not the doctrine of substitution, which has been misstated as the arbitrary punishment of one innocent man for guilty men, be relieved of some objections by an effort not to present a solution of it, but to

emphasize—after some words of comment—a Divine statement of the doctrine?

"His *voluntary* death," says Hooker, "prevailed with God, and had the force of an expiatory sacrifice." Voluntarily He partook of flesh and blood and took His place in the Judgment Hall, and when the accusing witnesses could not agree, and legally criminating testimony there was none, the August Victim by His own voluntary confession called down upon Himself the sentence of death, so that the Jews leading Him to Pilate said: "By our law He ought to die, because He *made* Himself the Son of God." He loved us, and gave Himself for us—How *willing* the Innocent One!

But then the Jews remind us of what in our thoughts on the atonement we often forget, that He was the Son of God, and these two things follow:

He is the God-Man, and He took to Himself "not some one person among men, but the nature which is common to all;" "since the children are partakers of flesh and blood He likewise took part in the same." There is no arbitrariness in the substitution. The nature that sinned was on the Cross. "Taking to Himself," says Hooker, "our flesh and by His Incarnation making it His own flesh He had now *of His own*, although *from us*, what to offer unto God for us." And then, too, because He is the Son of God it follows that the Divine Victim—the substitute came out of the Bosom of the Father to be propitiated, and God so loved the world that He gave Him. And whatever mystery there may be in the innocent suffering for the guilty, surely when the innocent victim comes forth in love and as the gift of love from the very Bosom to be propitiated, the Gift is worthy of all acceptation, the Giver worthy of all adoration. And one step more led by an Apostle's hand "God was in Christ reconciling the world unto Himself." The Innocent One is God in self-sacrifice for man's salvation. "This," says one whom I am glad to quote," is not Patripassion doctrine—it is the truth which the Patripassionist misstates." *

And now recall the Divine Statement of which I have spoken. It is St. Paul who speaks as moved by the Holy Ghost. He is looking at the atonement from above. We look at it too much from beneath.† St. Paul speaks as though caught up again to Heaven. "All things are of God," he says. The context shows that he speaks now of the "all things" not of creation, but of redemption: "All things are of God." God "hath reconciled

---

* Dr. Wm. R. Huntington.

† " If it might be said, without irreverence, the Catholic docrine thus teaches us to approach the Cross from above more naturally than from below."—CANON LIDDON.

us to Himself by Jesus Christ"—"All things are of God;" He "hath given to us the ministry of reconciliation"—"All things are of God"—"God was in Christ reconciling the world unto Himself"—"All things are of God"—God is "not imputing their trespasses unto them." "All things are of God—God hath committed unto us the word of reconciliation." "All things are of God." "God hath made Him to be sin for us who knew no sin, that we might be made the righteousness of "God in Him."* What, then, shall we say to these things? Is it not "our duty to render most humble and hearty thanks to Almighty God, our Heavenly Father, for that He hath given His Son our Saviour Jesus Christ to die for us." "We should always remember the exceeding great love of our only Saviour Jesus Christ thus dying for us."

3. The Catholic dogma of the Atonement includes also the third pair of complementary truths stated above. It includes a ransom *for the souls* of men, and yet a moral and mystical influence *on the souls* of men. On this point I must speak briefly. The Catholic doctrine of the Atonement admits and welcomes the most fervid word ever said on the moving, constraining, melting, regenerating life-giving power of Christ crucified. But it has equal and grateful welcome for the

---

* 1 Cor. v. 18–21.

truth that Christ on the Cross gave Himself a ransom *for* men—"redeemed" "bought them" by His blood. In his first Epistle St. John writes: "In this was manifested the love of God towards us, because that God sent his only-begotten Son into the world that we *might live through him.*" But in the next verse following he writes: "Herein is love, not that we love God, but that he loved us, and sent his Son to be the *propitiation for our sins.*"*

The doctrine of the Atonement here advocated is not a compromise, but a comprehension; it is not eclectic, but Catholic. The Church bows before the manifold mystery of the Atonement as she bows before the mystery of the Incarnation. Hooker has told us how "four most famous Ancient General Councils" have set forth the complementary truths with respect to the Person of our Lord, "in four words: *truly, perfectly, indivisibly, distinctly.* The first applied to His being God, and the second to His being man; the third to His being of both one, and the fourth to His still continuing in that one Both." No conciliar authority has put forth so comprehensive and concise a statement of the complementary truths of the Atonement. But probably every such truth, as may be seen by the quotations which follow, can be found in the Book of Common Prayer:

---
* St. John, iv. 18.

"Who for us men and for our salvation came down from Heaven and was *incarnate* by the Holy Ghost of the Virgin Mary, and was made man and was *crucified also for us* under Pontius Pilate." "Almighty God and *Most Merciful Father, who of Thine Infinite Goodness hast given* Thine Only and dearly beloved Son to be our Redeemer and the *author of everlasting life.*" "Almighty God, our Heavenly Father, who hast *purchased* to Thyself an universal Church by the *precious blood* of Thy dear Son." "Almighty God, who hast *given Thine Only Son* to be unto us both a *sacrifice for sin* and also an example of Godly life." "Almighty God, who hast given Thy only-begotten Son to *take our nature upon Him.*" "The Son of God did *vouchsafe to yield up His soul* on the Cross for your salvation." "O Saviour of the world, who by Thy Cross and *precious blood* hast *redeemed* us." "Help thy servants whom thou hast redeemed by Thy precious Blood." "If he believe that Jesus Christ hath suffered death upon the Cross for him and *shed His blood for his redemption.*" "They are the sheep of Christ, which He *bought with His death*, and for whom He shed His blood." "His *meritorious Cross and passion, whereby alone we obtain remission of sins* and are made partakers of the Kingdom of Heaven." "Who truly suffered, was crucified, dead and buried to *reconcile His Father* to us, and to be a *sacrifice* not only for original guilt, but also *for actual sins of men.*" "Through the *satisfaction* of Thy Son our Lord." "The offering of Christ once made is that perfect redemption, *propitiation,* and *satisfaction* for all the sins of the whole world, both original and actual; and there is none other *satisfaction* for sin but that alone."

II. That the revelation of the Atonement brings together with light mystery, that it presents complementary truths whose boundary lines we cannot adjust, is what we might expect. "Not only the reason of the thing, but the whole analogy of Nature, should teach us not to expect to have the like information concerning the Divine conduct as concerning our duty. Though we are sufficiently instructed for the common purposes of life, yet it is almost an infinitely small part of natural providence which we are at all let into. The case is the same with regard to Revelation. The doctrine of a Mediator between God and man relates only to what was done on God's part in the appointment and on the Mediator's in the execution of it. For what is required of us in consequence of this gracious dispensation is another subject in which none can complain for want of information."* To these words add the words of Lord Bacon: "We ought not to strive after a scheme of divinity which is perfect and

---
* Bishop Butler.

complete in all its parts. For he that will reduce knowledge into a scientific form will make it round and uniform; but in theology many things must be broken off, abruptly and concluded with, 'Oh, the depths of the wisdom and knowledge of God—how unsearchable are His jugdments and His ways past finding out.'" "The Mediator is the great mystery and perfect centre of all God's ways with His creatures." As we kneel before the Cross, we bow before the mystery of the Holy Incarnation—the mystery of the Holy Trinity. We hear the Mediator's first word upon the Cross: "Father, forgive them." Hours pass by, and we hear Him say: "It is finished." But meanwhile darkness has veiled the Cross. "What is going on beyond that darkened sky we see not."

III. In the next place may it not be claimed, for the complementary balance of truths here advocated, that by dealing more consistently than the logical systems of the Atonement with the Holy Scriptures, it does greater honor to the Scriptures. If in formulating my doctrine of the Atonement, I honor the Scriptures when they say, "God so loved the world," why should not I pay equal honor when they say, "The Son of Man came to give His life a ransom for many?" If I accept the words "He hath made Him to be sin for us who knew no sin," why should I not hear also the words "God was in Christ reconciling the world unto Himself?" What sort of consistency is that which bows before one deliverance of the witness, and turns the back upon another deliverance of the same witness upon the same subject? The principle of a truly Catholic Church is to "hear meekly" both testimonies, and "receive them with pure affection." And for that principle she reverently pleads the highest authority—the example of Him who, in the crisis of His temptation, to the words It is written, replied, "'It is written *again.*' It *is* written "He shall give His angels charge concerning thee, and they shall bear thee in their hands lest at any time thou dash thy foot against a stone." "And therefore," says logic, "cast thyself down." But there is a complementary truth. "It is *written again*" "Thou shalt not tempt the Lord thy God" by rash presumption. Our Lord did not deny that angels had charge concerning Him. Presently angels came and ministered to Him. But He balances the one Scripture against the other. What the gracious Head of the Church did with reference to the Old Testament the Church reverently does with reference to the Old Testament and the New. If tempted to go astray in doctrine by the words It is written, her reply is, It is written again. It is written "By the which *will* we are sanctified." But it is written again, "By the offering of the *Body* of Jesus Christ once for all." It is written in the Parable of the Lost Son, "The Father had compassion and ran and fell on his neck." But it is written again, "I am the Way and the Truth and the Life: no man cometh unto the Father but by me."

Still further, it is worthy of reverent notice that, in the volume of Scripture, He who said to His apostles: "I have many things to say unto you, but ye cannot bear them now," did say things which are germs of almost every leading truth in the Catholic dogma of the Atonement. He Himself gives the reason why He withholds many things—His apostles could not "bear them now." He spoke of suffering, death, resurrection; Simon Peter rebuked Him. And yet, apart from what He said of the Father's love and His Divine Sonship and union with man and renewal of man, listen to His words: "This is my Blood of the New Testament, which is shed for many for the remission of sins." "The Son of Man came to give His life a ransom for many." See how the "Notes" of Atonement are given in these words! Here is the "ransom;" here "substitution" is taught by the strongest of all particles. Here are "Blood," "Life," "Sins," "remission" —the "shedding of blood"—the "giving of His Life." Here high indeed the place in the mission of the Son of Man which is assigned to the gift of His Life for men: "He came not to be ministered unto, but to minister and to give His Life a ransom for many." May we not add the key-word of the Publican's prayer: "Be merciful"—be "propitiated?" Is there not here the germ and justification of the many witnesses to propitiation and reconciliation which testify in the pages of the Epistles?

IV. It is an argument for the Catholic doctrine of the Atonement; it gives it a pathetic meaning, that it fulfils with Divine fulness and tenderness the "unconscious prophecies of heathendom." It has seemed to be the almost universal conviction that the "method of delivering men's souls" must include expiatory sacrifice. It is declared to be notorious, the result of grave historical induction, that "all nations before the time of Christ entertained the notion that the displeasure of the offended deity was to be averted by the sacrifice of an animal, and that to the shedding of its blood they imputed their pardon and reconciliation;" that they were "as busy about sacrifice in the outer court of the Gentiles as in the holier place of the Jews." Unworthy were many of their sacrifices —even revolting. The Revelation, which tells us of God's infinite love and Gift and of the infinite worth of the Son of God, did not shine on them. What wonder if, groping in the darkness for some sufficient satisfaction for sin, they sometimes laid hands on and dragged to the altar some wailing virgin—some "fruit of their body for the sin of their soul?" Shall we involve in one contemptuous charge ("pagan") not only the special and ever-changing forms of expiation, but also the central idea of expiation and satisfaction, which seemed to voice the longing for the Cross? In an age which recognizes the teachings of the Divine Logos in the ethnic religions, we should recognize His Light in the prevalent and permanent practice of vicarious sacrifice. Doubtless those sacrifices were pointing though dimly to Calvary. Not only on Moriah's temple-crowned height, kindling in the light of Revelation and smoking with prophetic sacrifice did the cry ascend, Behold the Lamb of God! On many a mountain-top, where darkness covered the earth and strange altars were groaning with strange sacrifices there was heard the half-stifled cry: "Behold the Lamb of God!" Surely many such worshippers shall behold Him—behold Him in the land of perfect light and swell the Heavenly chorus, " Blessing and honor and glory and power unto the Lamb forever and ever."

What a reflection is that Heavenly vision of the glad adoration which now on earth we pay the Lord Jesus as the Lamb of God slain for us! How it justifies our reliance on the precious

Blood of Christ! "In Heaven it is around His Form as once pierced and bruised that the worshippers bend in adoration." "I beheld," says the Seer, "and lo! in the midst of the throne and the four living creatures and in the midst of the elders stood a Lamb as it had been slain. And the four living creatures and the four-and-twenty elders fell down before the Lamb, and sang a new song." And choristers from all creation gather to sing His praise—" rank encircling rank, and orb in orb." Angels' voices are heard, "ten thousand times ten thousand," and in the still widening choir is heard the voice of "every creature in Heaven and in earth and under the earth." New each song of adoration to the Lamb; the elders' song, the angels' song, the song of every creature. But this a theme of every song, the " Lamb as it had been slain;" this the opening strain that summoned from Heaven and earth the universal choir, " Thou hast purchased to God by Thy blood men of every kindred and tribe and people and nation."

Will you not permit me in conclusion to recur to my opening words—that the Catholic dogma of the Atonement is the " method of freeing men's souls."

Does not some such regulative law lie at the foundation of all human liberty? Political liberty has its regulative law—has for a foundation its dogmas, called a constitution. The intellect has its dogmas, the fundamental laws of thought; and the intellect has its freedom in obedience to them. In the realm of the mathematics he is the true freeman who, accepting the necessary truths as the charter of his intellectual liberty, goes forth to roam at will gladly and triumphantly from one starry province to another of this boundless universe. And if by spiritual freedom we mean the glad, spontaneous wide-ranging triumphant movement of the intellect and heart toward God, such a freedom as this is possible only for him who accepts the definite and dogmatic truth as it is in Jesus. That truth is adapted to man's nature. It responds to the cry of his heart. It fulfils his unconscious prophecies. It gives the propitiation he needs. It restores the lost order to the soul. It is the palladium of a liberty more precious than all other precious liberties—the liberty of the soul to look gladly out on the glory of the Lord and to be changed as it looks from glory to glory. It is the gift of the great Emancipator. "If the Son shall make you free ye shall be free indeed." Then will you have fallen into the ranks—I am using in part the words of another—you will have fallen into the ranks of that mighty movement of redeemed humanity, which, as it traverses the ages, follows the uplifted banner of the Cross, and when it would sing its hymn of human liberty repeats instinctively the Creed of the Apostles.

The Office and Work of the Holy Spirit.

LECTURE V.

THE OFFICE AND WORK OF THE HOLY SPIRIT.

THE RIGHT REV. DAVIS SESSUMS, D.D.,
Assistant Bishop of Louisiana.

THE subject committed to me is the Office and Work of the Holy Spirit. As it stands midway in the course, and presents the transition by which we pass from abstract to sacramental theology, it may be impossible to avoid repetition of something that has preceded or anticipation of something that may follow. Should such liberties of treatment exhibit themselves, I trust they may be pardonable, as involved in the nature of the subject.

Christianity has to do not only with the existence and with the revelation of God, but also with the possession of God by man. God is in Himself. He exists as in relation to man, and He also exists in man. He makes; He preserves; He perfects. He is the truth which man seeks —the only true way in which the search can be made; and He is also the life of the seeker. He is the end before, the law over, and the power within man.

I. The presence of God within the human individual, the participation of the divine which is realized for the mortal spirit by the Holy Spirit, is primarily assured to us in the fact that man is made in the image of God.

The imaging of the divine in the human is more than the reflection of an original in a copy. It is the vital extension into man of the being of God, so that the creature is the vehicle of the Creator's self-expression, and so represents Him that the Creator is known in the creature. A likeness to God cannot be an external resemblance, instituted in order that other beings may behold their Maker superficially, but must be an internal unification, by which man may know God immediately in his own spiritual faculties, and may become a means through which divine truth and divine life may be imparted.

In representing Himself in man, the Creator does not build a rival God, nor yet a lifeless effigy, but a vital revelation of Himself. His thought and feeling and will were to be so closely wrought into the inner history of His finite image that the latter's processes might, in the divine design, be held to declare His own. Human knowledge of God consists not in mere mental reflections of an object organically distinct from man's own personality, nor in notions concerning a truth which may be dissimilar to these notions themselves, nor in speculative and unreal ideas which might attest conversation, but not communication between man and God; but it is the realization, the translation of a divine presence, a divine fact in the very structure of man's own being. Truth, as we think it, is not a discovery of an external object, but it is God working in human faculties and permitting them to have at the same time the consciousness of a seeming independence, a seeming externality to Him. The evidence which man educes from himself concerning God is only his interpretation of the divine handwriting upon the spiritual walls of his own nature; it is only permitting God to speak for Himself in mortal speech. This immanence of God supplies man with a basis of religion in his own personality, enables his religion to be truly a personal religion, and liberates him from dependence upon outward evidences. The structural thought which he has of God needs not to be questioned, as though it required to be justified by proof outside of itself. Its presence in the mind is the truth which it represents actually and already present there, working itself into realization, constituting itself the beginning of that completer knowledge which may come by obedience, commanding acceptance because it is. When the mind, impelled God-ward by the deific impulse already within it, turns against the fact, and seeks to become external to this fact and to criticise it, the mental process loses in its doubt the very reality which it attempts to examine, suspends the very action of God which it is impatient to verify, destroys in the stagnation of criticism the very truth which is operating its own presence and confirmation. To blind one's self to ascertain whether one possesses eyesight is to slay the very faculty by which the assurance might be acquired. God, the immanent God, is the very self-certifying thought which moves in man's thought, seeking to reproduce there a divine consciousness. He is the very thought in which man thinks—the mind of his mind, the will of his will, life of his life, light of his light. God submits to be used, or to be abused.

True human thinking is not original, independent, absolute thinking; it is only that part of the divine thinking which human consciousness has admitted and appropriated. False thinking is free thinking. Man's true willing is only his conscious participation in the divine will, and his glory in creation and redemption is to interpret and communicate God. His sin is to misrepresent and expel Him. To close the being to God is to set man in isolation, to leave him a mind without a mind, a will without a will, a shell without a seed, eclipsing the very light by whose light he may see light. Thus to bar out God, thus to doubt Him, to turn from His manifested presence within the spiritual nature to the senses without, to condition obedience upon demonstration—this is to make abortive the fullest and the final effort of God; it is to sin the last and most fatal sin against the Holy Spirit.

God can do no more. He has entered into us and can come no nearer. He can give no more conclusive evidence than the gift to us of spiritual faculties already freighted with His presence. His resources are exhausted. He has enveloped us without and within.

Then to fail Him is, indeed, to fall upon bitterness and ruin. There is no mystical, unknown offence needed to send the Holy Spirit upon His everlasting flight. To make darkness where there is light is to abide in the night; and that self-blinding of the spirit which disowns God in disinheriting itself, which refuses worship when its own inmost being is a temple, overpowers Omnipotence, and sinks Him into depths of divine despair.

" For I say this is death, and the sole death,
When a man's loss comes to him from his gain,
Darkness from light, from knowledge ignorance,
And lack of love from love made manifest ·

A lamp's death when, replete with oil, it chokes ;
A stomach's when, surcharged with food, it starves.

" When man questioned, 'What if there be love
Behind the will and might, as real as they?'—
He needed satisfaction God could give,
And did give, as ye have the written Word ;
But when, beholding that love everywhere,
He reasons, ' Since such love is everywhere,
And since ourselves can love I would be loved,
We ourselves make the love, and Christ was not,'—
How shall ye help this man who knows himself
That he must love and be loved again,
Yet, owning his own love that proveth Christ,
Rejecteth Christ through very need of Him ?
The lamp o'erswims with oil, the stomach flags
Loaded with nurture, and that man's soul dies."

II. An ultimate danger involved in this conception of the internality of God is that of limiting the divine fact and act to the process realized in man. The final and subtlest form of Pantheism, arising from error along these lines, declares not only that God exists in human nature, but that He does not exist until and except in creation. It declares that He becomes personal only as man so becomes; that there is no self-existent object beyond the divine thought in the creature; that God is merely a name for the whole mind and feeling and will which are developed in mankind. But this misdirection of thought concerning the divine immanence should not obscure the fact that in this truth abide the utmost power and preciousness of Christianity.

The human consciousness is ever expressing or realizing itself in a threefoldness. Its structure is a trinity, a unity of self and not-self. But the consciousness of man cannot be the only consciousness, because it is ever increasing, extending, developing itself out of an infinite resource, supplying itself out of a previous intelligence, interpreting meaning universally, incessantly holding commerce with another Thought whose activity maintains in place and name objects which man may know and correlate.

Because human consciousness is progressive, and because it does not create but only obeys its own laws of logic, it must be taken to indicate the existence of a prior and authoritative logical method, which impresses itself upon man, and amid his waywardness testifies to an original and independent train of thought pervading the universe. The inner relation of the human to the divine is that of a recipient, upon whom the giver is endeavoring to pour out inexhaustible stores. The historical development of man, the inward pressure which impels the individual to growth, the whole subjective effort and aspiration of the spiritual life—these manifest the presence of God striving with and within humanity to find such free way, such outlet, that the creature may be expanded into His own existence. If it be said that the independence of God, His presence in finite image and the likeness between original divine being and derived human being cannot be demonstrated, it is to be answered that to doubt them is treason to consciousness itself. As ideas, as structural laws, as spiritual facts, they exist in man; and to attempt to penetrate behind them is to turn consciousness outside of itself, and to discredit the whole mental movement which accumulates science upon the basis of axioms. These spiritual facts exist; and to ignore them would be as arbitrary and destructive as to ignore their antitheses. The conclusions to which they lead are irrefragable, because they are essential to explain the phenomena of the inner life; and any system which denies them, in the effort to build the universe on the one strand of physical fact, is simply blinding itself to one entire half of that universe, and its theory is as illogical as disastrous. These spiritual facts find their confirmation, as all truth finds its proof, in experience; and they justify themselves in the fulfilment, the harmony, the reason which they impart to human life. To discover man's destiny in his likeness to God and his glory and inspiration in union with the divine nature is both revelation and science. To deduce infidelity from this glory is suicide.

III. Where it is even admitted that God is

truly God, and not the accretion of humanity, there may still be found a superficial acceptance of His existence as a bare, mechanical, arithmetical unit, instead of an organic unity, in which He may really bind creation to Himself. Such views, turning to an opposite extreme, consider God as purely external to man—as one dwelling in eternal solitude, without holding to that mystery of His nature by which he is connected with His creature. They contemplate God and man and nature in sheer independence and separateness— as though they constituted a succession of three contradictory entities; as though there obtained between them no relations save those of contiguity, of superficial contact, of tangential sympathy. They regard the divine activity as exerted only upon, and not in creation. Man's thought is here made a mere movement revolving about God, instead of a passage into Him; truth, mere mental imagery, instead of vital participation; revelation, a reflection upon the surface of humanity, instead of an incarnation in them; Trinity, three dissimilar units—God, nature, man— instead of the social constitution of the Godhead declaring itself in finite history. Such interpretations make man an outcast from God; reduce his spiritual experience to a fiction as under divine names without divine reality; and render impossible any true relationship between them.

Instead of magnifying man, as these views may strive to do, in some imaginary article of freedom, they empty him of God, and deny the unity which human thought demands in the cosmos. In some veritable sense, in some veritable way, all is one.

Either God is all in all, or there is no God. Organic unity is the only principle on which man can live and think in the universe. Either as from no God, all is the unity of materialism, or, as from God, all IS the unity of the Spirit. The independence and the immanence of God, God without and God within, as known both in Scripture and philosophy, are harmonized by an existence which enables Him to be both in Himself and in His creature. His nature must be such as to admit of this existence without self-destruction. His presence in the creature is not forced upon Him by the creature, but is the finite representation of an eternal fact within Himself. This immanence obtains because it corresponds to and is based upon the presence, within Himself, of both an original and a derived being. Through the relationship which God maintains with man is shadowed forth the fact of God relating Himself to Himself.

Behind the temporal son is the Eternal Son.

God is known as complete within Himself; keeping relations with Himself; having divine

Fact, divine Form, divine Force; eternal subject knowing Himself in eternal object, in unity; Origin, Expression, Relationship; Father, Son, Holy Spirit. The Father knows Himself in the Son, and is known by the Son; and God gives and receives, realizes and fulfils Himself in the Common Love, in the Holy Spirit, which moves from each to each, takes and returns, unites in distinguishing, and abides as the central Personality and medium of interchange between Father and Son. The possibility of finite creation lies in the fact of the Eternal Image in God. In Him as the Logos rests the divine participation of the universe—its extension along the lines of sonship, its secure membership in God. Here lies the truth of which Pantheism and Deism are equally misrepresentations. Creation is, indeed, divine, but not God. God is, indeed, Himself, but not selfish. Priority pertains to the Divine Subject, the Original Fatherhood who objectifies Himself in His Son, and so from Him primarily proceeds the Spirit. Yet the Eternal Love, the Unifier, moves reciprocally. In time, in history, the Holy Spirit is the Eternal Love of the Father bestowing itself upon man through the Divine Son, and the Eternal Love of the Son revealing for man's joy the glory which He and His members have in the bosom of the Father, and the Love of the Son gathering to itself the filial devotion of humanity, and returning in eternal loyalty to glorify the Father. Herein are indicated the subtle accuracy of the Eastern and the practical accuracy of the Western mind in divergent interpretations of the Procession.

IV. This Divine Unity, existing in self-relation, extending into the finite in both creation and redemption as essential to the expression of His own nature, is Perfect Personality. The mystery of the Godhead is not that of many fused into one, but of one in many, of Tri-personality, of Personality in diversity, of Unity in organic distinction. To realize a true unity in man's being; to admit humanity into the fulness of the divine fellowship, and open upon them the deeps of the divine nature; to fix a dwelling for the Godhead bodily in flesh; to admit the human creature through holy and holiest unto the very peace of God's inward self-communion—this is the gradual work of the Triune God. Lest man be overpowered, or play false and dishonor the sacred charge, he must first be bound to God by the Father, made to know the supremacy of God and the need of his own obedience. He may then be uplifted to filial freedom in the Son. And, finally, when secure yet free, the Holy Spirit may possess him fully, and touch him into sacred identity with the inner life of God; may establish him in fearless and unfaltering intimacy with the

Father as His true minister and the sharer of His joy and sovereignty. The successive work, the dispensations of God, do not signify that man's sin alone necessitated the elaboration of the Trinity—as though by human shame God were forced to sally forth from recesses wherein otherwise He would have held His eternal retreat, or man had come through the very ignominy of a fall to grasp a vaster blessing than his Maker originally designed. But they signify that the everlasting purpose of God to realize His image in humanity was not defeated by the apostasy of His creature; that God prevailed, though crucified by man. Thus complete in Himself, He works in time inseparably yet successively. And through the ages the Holy Spirit prepares for the mighty culmination of Pentecost; revealing more and more the life and law of the Father through the Son and inspiring the creature to rise to his birthright in the Kingdom of God.

V. In the physical order the Holy Spirit inaugurates the movement of life, causes living objects to develop in independence of the world of sameness around them, and enables organic being to arise. In the mystery of organism, where mechanical balance yields to the oneness which exists in complexity, where unity is found in variety, He suggests the mode of the Divine Being. Seeking final unification of God with the creature, working onward to humanity fulfilled in God, He evolves along the plan of the Eternal Form, in the logic of the Eternal Son, an ever-ascending series of life which prophesies the advent of man and of Christ. He interrupts here and there the sequence of the natural order, and indicates that its issue in the spiritual is not an accidental end attained by unconscious natural selection, but a predetermined conclusion of a divine design elaborated by the activity of the Lord and Giver of Life. He distributes throughout creation rudimentary forms of facts which perfectly exist in the second man—the Lord from Heaven—in order that the fitness of this latter to gather up and complete creation may be manifested; in order that He may be accepted by the creature as the satisfaction of his desire, the solution of his destiny. He combines, substance and form so that the visible world may communicate to man the beauty and order of the inner life of God. He broods over the natural man, and strives to elicit his consciousness of sonship in God. He is the spiritual presence, the spiritual power in the phenomenal, and gives to physical things a sacramental significance, establishing all formal existence of flesh and body and ceremony in the sanctity of a divine mission, exalting matter as the symbol and medium of incarnation, and preserving it from degradation by manichee and materialist. At last, in the fulness of time, He evolves the humanity of Christ, vivifying human flesh into form which should befit the Eternal Form of God; breaking the physical succession in order to effect a new spiritual beginning, and setting the mystery of a Virgin Birth over against the mystery of the origin of the first and natural man. The final man is given an embodiment which accords with his nature, and through a spiritual generation introduces the era of the Spirit—the reign of unity and love and the heavenly virtues.

VI. Within the human consciousness He works to produce some spiritual self, or gift, or character, or genius, by which the individual may become personal and independent; may realize an originality to be shared only with God, may represent some new divine truth to men. The aim is toward a personality whose knowledge and love and will shall resemble God's, above time and space and secondary cause. He pervades the Ego, the inward and most personal characteristic. Preserving responsibility, He yet seeks to develop in the human being and his history, through whatever faculty or activity of consciousness He can control, whatever divine fact that faculty or activity can represent. He inspires the movement in universal human mind toward cause and law and beauty, and through this natural inspiration He prepares for a higher and more spiritual, as human personality becomes more obedient to the Spirit that leadeth unto all truth. Degrees of this natural operation are seen in poets, philosophers, heroes, and great discoverers. But that which is technically and specially inspiration is that in the consciousness of man by which he has come to know his filial relation to God, has realized the mystery of the Triune Godhead, and has interpreted and applied the Incarnation. The Hebrew Prophets exhibit the fullest measure of this inspiration in the ages preceding Christ; the completest realization under the Spirit of the nature and purpose of God, of the divine destiny of man, of the progress of God's intention to extend, to incarnate Himself in human life and history. In them the Spirit moves onward in clearer and nearer approach to His perfect work. Finally, in Christ He fully enters into the ark of man's being; completes humanity in the image of God; inspires human nature, from its union with the Eternal Word, to enter into the reason of God; realizes for man in the consciousness of Christ the threefold mystery of Father, Son, and Holy Spirit; takes up the creature into the divine nature, and opens henceforth the possibility of a perfect peace, a real freedom, through filial obedience to the Father in the Unity of the Spirit. By this final work must be tested all that precedes and all that follows it. As thought and life, as the personalities of men harmonize with Christ, are they to be accredited to the Holy Spirit, and the measures and values of their inspiration to be determined. The persistence of the Prophets in their effort toward Him is evidence of the Spirit wrestling with them; and the results were conditioned by their individuality and responsibility. Both the divine economy and personal limitation affected the issues of their inspiration, and left them still humanly capable of development even in the exercise of their office. The delay of the consummation in Christ proceeds not only from the choice of God awaiting His own period, awaiting the fulness of time, but also from the fact that only then did responsible and obedient manhood enable the Spirit to enter upon. His full and unhindered dominion. Not only did God then dominate humanity by the power of His Spirit, but man by loyalty became capable of this divine expansion. The test of inspiration is not a law deduced from the Old Testament, but from Christ and the New, and thence applied to the Old. So far as the Old Testament is Christian, it represents the full technical work of the Spirit. Henceforth inspiration is still personal; but, as before it was not final in any unit, but in Christ, so now it is to be measured and accepted as realized in the Christ-

Body, the Church. When the work of the Spirit is not primarily to develop the consciousness in time relations, but eternally and toward God, it is illogical to expect that man, even as His vehicle, will be lifted above the necessities of growth or be severed from the influence of age and environment. God in giving Himself does not instantly unmake the human past, but constructs a new present and future. He does not by inspiration or incarnation change the laws which make man's progress personal as well as providential; He does not, by the gift of one truth, disentangle all error and fill up all gaps of ignorance. Though Christ and the Spirit have come, the old world is not immediately changed, nor is the new levelled to its grade; but the old is explored and interpreted and corrected in the light of the new, and is truly fulfilled in the law which makes the old to decrease as the new increases. The universal divine method is not to destroy the natural and the old, not to violate a rational transition to the spiritual and the new, by teaching these latter only in their own language and under their own forms, and utterly disembarrassed of the associations of their predecessors; but to give the spiritual and the new in terms of the natural and the old, troubling man with the likeness and the unlikeness, compelling him to sift and disentangle, and so providing him with results more real and valuable. The men of the Old Testament strove to search out the meaning of the Spirit; and amid much that is their own, of themselves and like themselves, there is much that is plainly above themselves, without parallel and without solution save in the Christ, and delivered by them as the servants of a Divine Ruler to whose mastery they bent in awe, but about whose final purposes they still perceived a veil. To this we cling: Their Messianic hope, their foreshadowing of the Word made flesh, their rising vision of humanity redeemed, unified, transfigured by membership in the one kingdom of the All-Father. It may not be possible to define the limits of the human and the divine in their work, as it is not possible in the old geologic world to identify all places and degrees where fire and force have wrought. Directing and developing a system which was to affect all ages and all mankind, the Spirit breathed through them, controlling and adjusting the effort of their personality to more infinite ends than they may have been enabled to apprehend. Moving them, He dominated their movement to be effectual in a larger plan than their individuality could have grasped or executed; behind the fragmentary realizations which He vouchsafed to human spirits there loom the sacred and mysterious proportions of a stupendous and unearthly design, the vast radiance of an over-ruling God, which no discoverable human element in the record of His instruments can weaken or obscure. The true Christian religion is not guilty of seeking to limit the range of the Holy Spirit, in His education of the world for and in Christ, to its own historical lines; nor does it travesty the method and fact of inspiration by approximating it to the pagan idea of a supposed supernaturally intoxicated frenzy producing mechanically perfect, yet dubious oracles; nor does it, because human beings are thought to exhibit, or do exhibit, fallibility on some subjects, practise an indiscriminate and illogical denial of their divine calling and authority on all other subjects. But it is certified of God's victorious work, when it finds the superhuman amid the demonstrably human; it maintains the moral value of revelation and religion by preserving the responsibility of the instrument; and it obtains confirmation both by its likeness and its unlikeness to ethnic inspiration. The work of the Holy Spirit, as the inspirer, is progressive; it increases; it does not diminish. The new is nearer to Christ than the old, as clear truth is greater than prediction, as gift is more than promise. The revelation of God to the Apostles was not limited to the ancient books, but was fulfilled in His gift to their living selves. And the revelation to the Church was not limited to what its founders recorded, but was to be fulfilled in the living body of the Church, as it should be led by the Spirit. The Word of God was in human flesh, and the oracles of God are in the Church—in the spirits of men united in Christ under the tuition of the Spirit. The living Church, in its unity, is not only keeper but Interpreter of Holy Scripture. It is the sacramental fact of the Incarnation, and is therefore the pillar and ground of this latter's truth. The body of Christ bearing in its own hand its Bible, its ancestral record, its family chart, neither expects men to solve the biographical meaning without its teaching, nor fears any flaw which ingenuity may detect in the documents; for itself abides as both the key and the final defence of Christianity. Even when criticism claims to have reduced the Bible to the level of the ethnic religions, and by equalization with them to have disproved its inspiration, it has only succeeded in saying that certain common phenomena underlie the universal religious life of man. The conclusion is not to negative divine inspiration, but to assert that God in some way has had witness in all nations, and to multiply proofs of the necessity and the fact of the Incarnation. The very effort toward God is from God. That it was no part of Christ's endeavor to reorganize man out of error into truth instantly, nor to deal with him from the standpoint of an infallible mind impatient of man's biassed logic, is shown by the gradual expression of His own consciousness of Incarnation, by its culmination in His post-resurrection body, by His prophecy of the more absolute truth and the more final divine method which were to be introduced by the Holy Spirit.

VII. Since in Christ was accomplished the perfect work of God upon man; since in Him the divine end and way and power had all been safely lodged in human nature, and the meaning and use of the in-dwelling God had been guarded by the revelation of the object and the method which man should pursue; since in Christ humanity had been permitted to discern the effect of the Spirit, had been supplied with a means by which they could be certified of the actuality and the law of the work of the Spirit—it then became possible for the Spirit to be spread abroad in mankind, for God fully to possess His creature. The breath of the Almighty then filled humanity; the full divine glory settled upon manhood; the overwhelming weight and process swept in, and the full Power and Love of God are intrusted to His mortal image. God had waited long enough, and at last the Heavenly Dove returned to His rest. If man is faithless to this Holy Guest and fails to answer in love this gift of love, then the ignominy of his ingratitude touches its climax, and henceforth he can know no consolation. The goal toward which He seeks to develop man, the pattern into which He would mould him, the treasure He would bestow—these all are stored in the Christ. In Him is the exhaustion of divine beneficence; and in Him the fruition of man's devotion and might. In Him are fulfilled divine purpose and human effort. The Spirit must take of His and manifest Him unto men; distribute unto them the truth of the Incarnation, and enable them to realize Christ. He must awaken in man the sense of sonship, elaborate in him a revelation, convince him that he is doomed to union with God. To achieve this, to build this spiritual glory actually into our manhood as it is in Christ; to exalt the mortal to participate in the unity which Christ has with God; to enable him to say, "Abba," "Father," and to live in the splendor of the liberty of the sons of God; to have mankind transfigured in a divine commission which ennobles them and uplifts them into companionship with the Everlasting Father, until even their humanity seems to assume a new and mysterious nature in its union with the Eternal Son of God—to achieve this is the final salvation, the infinite blessedness which make the mission and the greatness of Christianity. Because the Holy Spirit has established in Christ the sign and measure of His operation,

He then proceeds to enter into all humanity, to pervade individuals, to realize in the units of the race what is contained in the Generic Head. Connecting mankind with Christ; representing, repeating in the Church, as organically one with Christ, an existence like that in which Christ dwells; He constitutes the Church the ideal, the universal man, the race made one in Christ, wherein the Holy Spirit dwells completely.

Through this body He gradually moves into men. Employing it as a centre organized into unity by Himself, He protects Himself against vagaries of individualism, and yet multiplies the points of contact from which He shall touch mankind. The Church thus becomes the Apostle, the "One sent of God" to extend the Incarnation, to effect salvation by incorporating humanity into filial relationship with God. Its very nature, essence, and function are to represent, to declare, to realize the atonement and the At-Onement, the forgiveness of sins in the actuality of organic membership in Christ, and the realization of a positive spiritual holiness; to take men into that connection with God in which they find mercy as sons, and in which their righteousness may become a participation of God; to constitute a state of being which shall witness the manifested love of God in the realized unity with Himself of His faithful sons; to present before men and to be to men a fact in which they are out of wrath and in the development of the divine life. Again, the Church is Apostolic because its whole being began as a full creation, as a complete organism, with the Apostles instituted as the essential official factor of its constitution; because the Apostolic order was not an evolution from the Church, but even while representing the character of the Body it still existed by independent appointment from Christ; because the Apostolic order, gathering the Church around itself, perpetuates the historical witness to the Resurrection of Christ; because through the Apostles and their successors, through the continuity of an historical office, divine fact is defended against the lawlessness of subjective speculation, and an objective witness is established by God Himself to the priestly mission of human nature, to the purpose which forever seeks to communicate God to man through man. It possesses the means of assurance that it is in connection with the Spirit, the educational media operated by the Spirit to build it into Christ, and the historical witness that the Spirit is at work within it; and it has the means of imparting its divine gift to the nations, of communicating to humanity membership in its divine heritage.

The unity of men with God under the Spirit operates unity of man with man, and is to be represented in time by a progress toward social unification, by a progress toward that universal brotherhood which may realize the Kingdom of God and such pure truth as may underlie the Utopias of philosophers and the dreams of Socialism; by a progress toward that pure society where man shall be in love with man, and where competition shall be only a rivalry of beneficence between human souls consciously intrusted for each other with good gifts from God. Because the Spirit of truth is in the Church, in the unity of the Church there abides an inspiration to discover and to teach the truth; to develop in the catholic mind of the Body of Christ the Mind of God; to realize an accumulation of truth which accords with, but is not limited to, the past; to enable the United Church to comprehend the Bible in the light of the Spirit, and to make its utterance the final and divinely representative voice upon the truths of religion. The same Spirit who empowers the Church of God to prepare and preserve its recorded biography in the Bible is still in the living Church, and seeks forever to realize in humanity the full consciousness of God, until this humanity in Christ shall know God as God is known by the Living Son, who is the Living and Eternal Word. In the Church the Holy Spirit works to effect amid men a visible Communion of Saints, instead of a theoretical sentimental sympathy; an organic body expressing itself in symbols, interpreting itself as the end of human existence, as the heavenly society of beings who are one in God, yet preserved in personality, instead of a temporal vehicle for transmitting select souls to a selfish paradise beyond itself; a unity which will repeat in time the mystery of unity in diversity, as God is One yet not solitary. He seeks to establish a communion of Christians who strive in love to be of one mind in order to receive the sure gifts of God, instead of petty sectaries striving to vindicate against each other selfish and individual dogmas. The Communion of Saints, as the Spirit moves in the life of the Church, is both an ideal and a progress. It is not the company of the favorites of God who are exempt from penalty and saved as Pharisees, but are children growing in grace, whose sainthood is the privilege and practice of the Christian life; whose glory is not a freedom from responsibility through perfected holiness, but whose holiness increases as they manifest the love of God, and become themselves its witnesses to men; who are saints and saved because they follow Christ in watching and waiting and working for the redemption of man. By binding men to Christ, the Spirit unifies them together and makes into one fellowship with Him all the family of God, living and departed, past and present.

As they grow into Christ they grow into each other, and all must participate in the life and work and joy of all; until salvation is realized as the corporate blessedness of the Body of Christ, until the individual exists alone in neither joy nor pain, until the need of the body is fed by each single member, and the member in his weakness is sustained in time and eternity by the body. Fulfilling His mission as the Bearer of Peace, He effectuates and completes the forgiveness of sins by imparting a new being, in which the need of forgiveness may pass away; by establishing not a negative release from the effects of broken law, but a positive gift and power of righteousness; by achieving not a removal of barriers, but a growth and development of man's being into actual unity with God—not merely a declaration of mercy from God, but a transformation of man into the likeness of divine righteousness. The Spirit labors to give life not only to the natural body, but also to the spiritual body; to make the formal life of man accord with the spiritual; to evolve out of the material in which God has planted man the full man in spirit and body; to produce that resurrection body which shall realize a unity of being for man —a perfect word for a perfect thought, a perfect form for a perfect fact, a perfect body for a perfect spirit.

VIII. The eternal life is that life which the Holy Spirit develops in man in likeness to the divine—the life wherein the faculties which are directed toward God act as He acts; where, as God in the Spirit has entered man in His own fulness and unity, man's life is enabled to become a true presentation of God; where the spiritual quality and character of man increase and widen his relationship to God in Christ. This life is laid not in distinctions of time and duration, but in fellowship with God—in independence of distinctions of time and space, in timelessness, in absolute existence like God's, in being because God is. Here the idea of destructibleness passes away, and the persistence of the human being is involved in the unity of his life with God. The Being of God carries that of His creature. The life, the living in God, opens into past, present, and future, and exists continually. This life neither gives nor needs proof of immortality, because it is conscious of it in its own oneness with the life of God, and has its eternal joy in knowing and realizing God in His love. The influence of the Holy Ghost transforms religion from the service of an external God and Law-giver into co-operation with a Father for a common end; moves man to know God as Love, and to comprehend His law as the expression of His love; enables him to call God a friend, and to seek a destiny which shares the divine glory and lifts him into the intimacy of a natural companionship. It moves him to interpret God's law not only as exterior commandment, but as equally the ideal of his own desire, and makes his obedience an irresistible sympathy instead of an enforced observance. It inspires him to feel that the aim of his being is not to obey God for an end wholly independent of himself, but to express out of his own spirit a love for God which is its own self-impelling law, and which constrains the life to an invincible devotion. It presents God as a Person, and by creating a profound fellowship with Him makes man unconscious of any limit to obligation, and drives him in utter fidelity to lose himself in order that the will of God may be done and His goodness be declared. It takes man out of the kingdom of nature, out of the fact of the Fall, out of the fear of failure and sin, and lifts him into the Kingdom of God, where he shall know in himself the positive possibilities of goodness and the impulses which flow from the consciousness of a divine birthright; where he may grow in the fearlessness of filial love into the greatness of his inheritance.

Under the administration of the Spirit, the new powers and new knowledge which rise in human nature constitute an ever-present witness to the resurrected and ascended Christ; and the summons to man to fulfil the work of Christ reveals the glory to which God has called him. Since Pentecost the divine method with humanity has not been to condescend to them as outcasts, deprived of likeness to the Father, but to unfold in them that eternal spiritual capacity which can make them actual sharers of His nature. He has poured out His Spirit upon all flesh, and henceforth in the religion of the Incarnation the human being is consecrated in the mystery of a divine companionship; his objects are transfigured with the greatness of the divine purpose, his mind is illumined to think God's thoughts after Him, his sacrifices are revelations of the divine love, his tongue is touched with the fire of an authoritative message; and as a possessor of the Holy Spirit he is lifted into the holy company of Martyrs and Prophets and Apostles.

Grace and the Sacramental System.

LECTURE VI.
GRACE AND THE SACRAMENTAL SYSTEM.

THE REV. G. H. S. WALPOLE, D.D.

Professor of Systematic Divinity and Dogmatic Theology in the General Theological Seminary.

THE subject of which I am to speak this evening presents no small difficulty when looked at in relationship to the main trend of men's thoughts to-day.

At a time when the powers of this world are being generally regarded as adequate for all men's necessities, grace points to a supernatural force.

At a time when the intellect is claiming to be the sole means through which spiritual development may be perfected, grace points to certain humble instruments which, by their very simplicity, disclaim educational value as their chief merit.

At a time when religious individualism is rampant, the power of fellowship everywhere disregarded, even the bond of family prayer set aside, grace points to a Mediatorial Kingdom, through which alone man can arrive at his perfection.

Sacramental Grace,* then, in the idea it presents, challenges the ground of that buoyancy which is the characteristic feature of our times. For indeed, in spite of the fires of discontent which lie smouldering beneath the thin crust of that surface life which is chronicled every day for us in our daily journals, humanity as represented by its thought is proud and confident. The golden age of general prosperity is supposed to be almost within hail. Disease after disease is disappearing before the touch of medical science, blot after blot is being removed from the moral code, social inequalities are being adjusted, and a reign of universal peace is setting in.

To quote Mr. Fiske's words, "Man is slowly passing from a primitive social state in which he was little better than a brute toward an ultimate social state in which his character shall have become so transformed that nothing of the brute can be detected in it. The ape and the tiger will become extinct. The modern prophet, employing the methods of science, may again proclaim the Kingdom of Heaven is at hand." Into such

---

* I have not discussed the question of the various meanings attached to the word "Grace" in the New Testament, as the title of the lecture sufficiently indicated what particular sense I was to attach to it.

a glowing prophecy of the ultimate issues of natural forces, it would seem almost an impertinence for the subject of sacramental grace to intrude itself, were it not that men are unable to find rest in these great promises for the race. Men are everywhere asking, "But what of us?" If you tell us that it cannot be proved that there is *not* another world, nay, that "it is quite likely science does not give us the whole story, and that death may be but the dawning of true knowledge and true life," then we ask, How are we to be fitted to stand the bright light of that great sunrise? The race may emerge in the distant future from its brute inheritance, but how are we as individuals to be free of it? As a proof of this eager questioning, see the remarkable evidence afforded by pleasure-loving Paris,* where the Christian faith stands encompassed with many infirmities and facing a hostile government and popular prejudice. And yet there are to be found in the old historic Church of Notre Dame, every week of this Lenten season, nearly three thousand men of the most educated classes of society, and in a neighboring parish church nearly one thousand men, chiefly of the working class, waiting to find some answer to this pressing question of their

---

* See the account of the Lenten Conferences and services held in Paris during the Lent of 1891, and published in the *Guardian* newspaper.

souls. It is not different here or elsewhere. In spite of the press of business, or the labor of mechanical work, the old question, "How may I save my soul?" or, to put it in a modern dress, "How may I be fitted for that dawn of true knowledge and true life?" is still imperious in its demand. The subject of sacramental grace, which has an answer to this question, cannot then be out of place.

But further, looking at the subject in its relation to the course of which it is a part, we see that it naturally forms a fitting conclusion to that series of dogmas that has been presented to us. Humanity was taken into God, reconciled to the Father, indwelt by the Holy Ghost that it might be perfected by the impartition of the Divine nature.

Perfection—yes, that is the purpose of the extraordinary condescension of God manifested in the Incarnation; and it is this we must first consider, or the need and particular virtue of grace may be imperfectly comprehended. If God's ultimate object with us were but the change of our circumstances, earth for heaven, then indeed we might fail to see the necessity of grace; but if it be full completed growth after such a measure as "the stature of the fulness of Christ," then how can we attain without it? The throwing off the brute inheritance were much; but the likeness to Christ is something more, preaching as it does the highest courage, the most unfaltering loyalty, the most complete devotion to God and man.

Perhaps we can best grasp the future that is held out to us, if we look at some of the powers which Revelation tells us will be committed to our hands. Characterized as our life is by weakness, we can hardly take in the visions of future strength that are shown us. We see One radiant in glory and power, no longer subjected to weakness, infirmity, or suffering, with a Body like unto ours save that it is infinitely ennobled and glorified, appearing here or there according to will, controlling the powers of nature, overriding by some higher law the ordinary laws of our world, finding no obstacle in matter, ascending into the heavens. And as we look, we are told that our bodies are to be fashioned like unto His glorious body, that they are to be raised in power, glory, and honor; and that we shall be "like Him, for we shall see Him as He is."* And then, looking away from this "exceeding and eternal weight of glory,"† as St. Paul calls it—a glory surpassing our present humiliation immeasurably more than the most gorgeous flower surpasses the dull brown seed from which it sprang,— looking away, I say, to those visions that are given

---
* Phil. iii. 21. 1 John iii. 2. † 2 Cor. iv. 17.

us of the "divine offices that suit these full-grown energies," we find ourselves immersed in the marvellous activity of a great city life, undertaking duties that here we cannot dream of, having authority given us over two, five, ten cities; sitting in judgment over angels, having power over the nations, ruling them with a rod of iron—nay, sharing the very throne of the Lord Himself.*

As our imagination attempts to fill in these splendid outlines of wonderful spheres of influence, we learn the necessity of grace, for we ask who is sufficient for these things? It is clear we must be changed—but how? The best education earth can afford, its most stimulating examples are all unequal to develop such spiritual power, such iron strength, such a wide and sovereign influence as is here spoken of.

And this necessity becomes still more apparent when we have the courage to look steadily at our present condition. Conscious of a will that swerves at the most trifling discomforts, of a mind that can scarcely contemplate God or heaven for an hour together, of a spirit so weak that it fails to move even children, we feel that that high destiny cannot be ours—we grow despondent; we assent at once to Shelley when he cries:

> The Universe
> In Nature's silent eloquence declares

---

* Luke xix. 1 Cor. vi. 3. Rev. ii. 26, 27. Rev. iii. 21.

That all fulfil the work of love and joy—
All but the outcast man—

We sadly recognize the truth of Byron's words:

> How beautiful is all this visible world,
> How glorious in its action and itself:
> But we, who name ourselves its sovereign, we,
> Half dust, half deity, alike unfit
> To sink or soar, with our mixed essence, make
> A conflict of its elements and breathe
> The breath of degradation, and of pride,
> Contending with low wants and lofty will
> Till our mortality predominates,
> And men are—what they name not to themselves
> And trust not to each other.

We feel the power of the Scripture assertions: "That which is born of the flesh is flesh;" "All have come short of the glory of God;" "There is none that doeth good—no, not one;" "Who can bring a clean thing out of an unclean?" And yet though we feel we cannot rise, we refuse to sink. "Half dust" we know ourselves to be and yet "half deity," we cannot help hoping we may become. The prophetic vision surpasses our capabilities, and yet strangely enough exceeds not our hopes. With its unshaken loyalty, and its mighty wide-reaching influence, it calls up before the imagination a "great gulf fixed;" and yet, when the judgment condemns the leap to be suicidal, the heart will not be deterred from attempting it.

Ah! there is nothing more pathetic in man's

history than this perpetual struggle between our baser selves and our divine hopes. "Pride contending with low wants and lofty will till our mortality predominates." "Alike unfit to sink or soar."

But we ask, Is this our only revelation? Can we reach no further than this humiliating confession that grace is necessary? "Surely," we say, "He who has given the hope will enable us to attain it." And so we find, for in the Incarnation we have the pledge of it. In that divine uplifting of human nature, the possible perfection of all that bears the name of man is assured. The Eternal Son can henceforth account nothing human as foreign to Him.

The knowledge of this great fact braces our wills and kindles our hopes; but knowledge is not sufficient for this huge task that lies before us. Knowledge cannot bridge over that wide gulf. It is not enough to know that we may hope. Our ignorance is not the worst thing about us. There is something worse than ignorance, and that is a perverted nature. St. Paul had knowledge, but he confesses its weakness. He declares that he knew that God's will was spiritual,—nay, that his inward man delighted in it,--but he found another law in his members warring against the law of his mind and bringing him into captivity,*

---

* Rom. vii. 22, 23, 24.

and in an agony he cries out: "Who shall deliver me from the bondage of this death?"

This "law in his members" was the law of nature and nature is stronger than knowledge. This is seen, I think, if we compare their effects upon our destinies here. Let us look at this for a moment. Compare the effects of nature and what we call education, upon one's destinies here. The infant, when it utters its first cry, seems as far off its earthly destiny as we from our heavenly. What sign is there that those baby fingers that can scarce hold a feather may awake thousands to a world before closed to them? What likelihood that that voice so harsh may one day hold multitudes spell-bound? What probability that that mind scarcely conscious may weave thoughts that will stir generations unborn? Wherein, humanly speaking, lies the best hope of the fulfilment of its destiny? On its education or on that nature it inherits from its parents? We need not stay long in our answer. There is a presumption that the musician's son will find out fresh secrets in the world of music; there is a possibility that the orator's son will show some power of eloquence; there is a probability that the offspring of a great thinker will master some new fields of thought. This we freely recognize. But, on the other hand, we do not look for a Mozart from the Patagonian, nor a Nathaniel Hawthorne from the Syrian, nor a Shakespeare from the Australian black. It is true that science has not yet told us by what law this probability exists as a probability; but we recognize it as a fact. We call it the law of heredity.

And this mysterious law affects not only what we call talents, but in a more universal way character. Judge Patteson and his saintly wife enriched the world with the martyr, John Coleridge Patteson; Margaret, the poor "gutter-child" of the upper Hudson, impoverished it by her descendants, of whom no less than two hundred are said to have been criminals.* This subtle, unseen power of nature, acting in ways we know nothing of, predetermines character, gives it a set, a prejudice, a bias; and it is terrible to know that, so far as our spiritual destiny is concerned, this prejudice is for death rather than life. "In Adam all die,"† is the sad exclamation of the Apostle. "Death reigned from Adam to Moses, even over them that had not sinned after the like ness of Adam's transgression."‡ We are then here confronted with a greater and more powerful obstacle to the realization of our destiny than ignorance, an obstacle which knowledge cannot remove.

---
* Herbert Spencer: "Man *versus* the State," p. 69.
† 1 Cor. xv. 22. ‡ Rom. v. 19.

This is even admitted by one whose only gospel was culture, whose only weapon was education. A late leader of the Positivist School in England (Mr. Cotter Morrison) frankly admits that for some there is no remedy at all.*

"There are some soils," he says, "which no farmer in his senses would think of ploughing, manuring, and sowing. There are kinds of vegetables and stocks of cattle which are recognized as unfit for profitable culture. It is the same with human qualities. There are men whose quality is to manifest from their earlier years a bias to vicious and malignant crimes; there are men whose bias is in the contrary direction. And these differences are congenital. We may be sure that no moral training will ever turn the bad into good, the evil constitution into the vigorous and moral. Nothing is gained by disguising the fact that there is no remedy for a bad heart and no substitute for a good one. The sooner we recognize that bad men will be bad, do what we will, the sooner we shall come to the conclusion that the welfare of society demands the suppression or elimination of bad men. It has a right not only to exclude them from its fellowship, not only to prevent and punish their evil actions, but above all to prevent their leaving a posterity as wicked as themselves."

---
* "Service of Man," pp. 290-295.

This is the witness not only of a polished thinker, but of a man who loved humanity: the very sentences I have quoted occur in the book which he entitled the "Service of Man;" and with him Mr. Herbert Spencer appears to agree. A time may come again when some enlightened Pharaoh will commend to his government the policy of destroying the children of a criminal population lest they "become too strong."

The world, then, speaking through one of her able thinkers, regards nature in certain cases as so much stronger than knowledge that some individuals it would destroy for the service of the state.

Now it has always been the singular merit of the Church, that though she has forced her way into the dark places of the earth she has never regarded any as being too bad to be reformed. Both in theory and practice she has thrown her gates wide open to the poor lepers of society. By her penitentiaries, her homes for the fallen, the outcast and the inebriate, she proclaims everywhere that none need despair who enter her doors—that there is healing medicine for the worst.

And on what does she rely? Does she look to that weapon which the world, as we have seen, confesses in some cases to be useless? Does she rely on the powerful preaching of the Word, on inspiring pictures of the love of God, on all the varied instruments of education? Not mainly. She uses them as God-given means for awakening the soul to its need; but she does not expect to satisfy the need itself with them. For this she relies on grace. It was, as Hooker * reminds us, an old gnostic heresy, " that had knowledge in such admiration that to it they ascribed all and so despised the sacraments of Christ—pretending that, as ignorance had made us subject to all misery, so the full redemption of the inward man and the work of our restoration must needs belong unto *knowledge only.*" No, the Church looks to "the grace of our Lord Jesus Christ." "I believe in one Baptism for the remission of sins." This is her proclamation in the East and West—in the old world and the new. It was her first, as we believe it will be her last.

When, as a new creation but a few hours old, she faced the great world in the plenitude of her inspiration, she replied to the anxious question, "What shall we do?" † with but two directions: " Repent and be baptized, every one of you in the Name of Jesus Christ for the remission of sins, and ye shall receive the gift of the Holy Ghost."

How, indeed, could she do otherwise? She had no other commission. But a few days back, she

---
* Hooker: "Eccles. Polity," v., lx. 4.
† Acts ii. 38.

had received from her Lord, who stood in the midst of her, this great charge:

"All power is given unto Me in Heaven and upon earth.

Go ye, therefore, and make disciples of all the nations,

Baptizing them into the name of the Father and of the Son and of the Holy Ghost.

Teaching them to observe all things, whatsoever I commanded you.

And, lo! I am with you all the days, even unto the end of the world."

The words speak of an external power, the exercise of which depends on Christ's Presence.

The stern Roman, the cultured Greek, the lascivious Asiatic, the wild, ignorant cunning Arab, were to be brought to the feet of their Master, to become His disciples and to learn His mind and to be possessed of the secret of His great life, not by an inspiring example, not even by knowledge in the first place, but by grace.

Mr. Morrison, the Positivist, rightly says: "There must first be some original quality to begin upon. Cultivation is only rationally applied where there is original quality capable of receiving it." This is the teaching of the Lord Christ—Baptism into the Name first, teaching second; grace first, knowledge second.

This doctrine, new as it may seem to some to-day, was not new to the Apostles. For three years our Lord had been impressing on their minds but two great truths—man's need; God's grace.

The first He excited by drawing such a picture of man at his best that even to-day it excites the enthusiasm of the world.

The Sermon on the Mount has been accused of being impracticable, an impossible ideal; but no one has charged it with being imperfect.

With that highest standard, "become perfect even as your Father in heaven is perfect," He left men to feel their need; and when human nature confesses its powerlessness and cries out in despair: "If this is to be my standard, who then can be saved?"* He reminds it that "With men it is impossible, but with God all things are possible."

Men are quite right in charging the standard of Christ as an impossible human standard, if by this they mean that man cannot reach it by himself. It is only what our Lord Himself says again and again: "That which is born of the flesh is flesh. Apart from Me ye can do nothing." But while teaching men their absolute impotency in words that cannot be explained away, He shows equally clearly that there is a power now within the reach of all men which will accomplish all that is set before them.

---
* Mark x. 27.

The Kingdom of God in its life, its powers, its extraordinary privileges, is beyond the effort of the greatest natural genius—nay, beyond a John the Baptist; but he who is born of water and of the Spirit at once enters within the circle of its life-giving blessings.*

The life which is called everlasting life, with its supreme devotion to God, its unwearying sympathy with man, not only seems, but is beyond the grasp of human powers, and yet "he that eateth the flesh of the Son of man and drinks His blood" has it.† "The life dwells in him and he in the life." Nothing could be plainer than this language. Whatever may be meant by birth, whatever by "the Flesh and Blood of the Son of man," it is only by realizing their meaning that we can gain what we seek.

Now it is at once plain that something more mysterious is intended by these phrases than that which we may call the results of Christian education, or preaching. To assert that by birth we mean simply what we call conversion—*i.e.*, a change or development of life already existing—is not only to assert that our Lord purposely used difficult language instead of plain language, but to contradict, as Hooker ‡ points out, every ancient interpretation of the passage. And Dr.

---

* Luke vii. 28.   John iii. 5.   † John vi. 54, 56.
‡ "Eccles. Polity," v., x. 3.

Dale,* the eminent Congregationalist minister, uses still stronger language. " Such a description is theologically false and practically most pernicious and misleading. Regeneration is not a change in a man's life, but the beginning of a new life, which is conferred by the immediate and supernatural act of the Holy Spirit. The man is really born again. A higher nature comes to him than that which he inherited from his human parents. He is begotten of God—born of the Spirit."

It is not easy to give any other than the Catholic meaning to our Lord's words to Nicodemus, but it is still more difficult to interpret in any other way His words to the men of Capernaum.

Here again we may not only appeal with confidence to the Catholic writers of the Church at all times and in all places, but be helped by the clear, strong statement of the Protestant, Prof. Godet, one of the greatest living commentators on the writings of St. John. This is the witness of this Swiss pastor of Neuchatel:

" If the words 'except ye eat the Flesh of the Son of Man and drink His blood'† refer to the purely spiritual idea of appropriating His holy life, of believing in His atoning Death, does He not

---
* "Lectures on the Ephesians," pp. 44-46.
† Godet, St. John vi. 58.

seem to be playing upon the words, and giving needless cause of offence to the Jews? There is no figure of speech except in the expressions 'eat and drink'—the corporeal side of communion with Him is perfectly real and must be taken literally."

Now what do these interpretations mean? What does Dr. Dale mean by the words "a higher nature comes to us," and Prof. Godet by the words "the corporeal side of communion with Christ is perfectly real and must be taken literally."

What do they mean but what Hooker* has so well said, that "Adam is in us as an original cause of nature, and of that corruption of nature which causeth death, Christ as the cause original of restoration to life. As therefore we are really partakers of the body of sin and death received from Adam, so except we be truly partakers of Christ and as really possessed of His Spirit, all we speak of eternal life is but a dream."

Yes, " By grace we are saved through faith, and that not of ourselves; it is the gift of God." † So the prophetic foresight of Plato, that we are allured to virtue not by teaching, not by our own nature, but by the influence of the gods, is now realized by the fulfilment of the blessed promises of Christ.

---

* Hooker, v., lvi. 8. † Eph. ii. 8.

For by "grace" we mean, as has been said,* "not what the witty and free-thinking gentlemen of Bishop Berkeley's day represented it as being— nothing but an empty name—but an active spiritual force."

By grace we mean, not simply kindly feeling on the part of God, but, as Dr. Liddon † has put it, "the might of the Everlasting Spirit renovating man by uniting him whether immediately or through the sacraments to the sacred manhood of the Word incarnate." The effect of grace, then, is not that of a picture on the mind, or of words on the ear, but, to use Hooker's ‡ words, "a real transmutation of our souls and bodies from sin to righteousness, from death and corruption to immortality." And so we understand those expressions of which the New Testament is full, to be statements of fact and not mere metaphorical expressions.

We believe that St. Paul,§ when he said that Christ lived in him and he in Christ, meant something more than that he was permeated by the genius of Christianity; we believe that St. Peter,‖ when he declared that through the realiza-

---

* Paget: " Faculties and Difficulties for Belief and Disbelief," p. 193.
† " Univ. Sermons," 1st series, p. 44.
‡ Hooker ' Eccles. Polity," v. 67, 6.
§ St. Paul, Gal. ii. 20. ‖ 2 Peter 1. 4.

tion of Christ's promises we become partakers of the Divine nature, meant something more than that "we live and move and have our being" in God; we believe that when St. John speaks of "abiding in Christ," "having Christ," "being begotten of God," he is meaning something more than is intended by a mere faithful contemplation of the Saviour; we believe that where He is spoken of as "the Second Man"—"the last Adam,"* we are intended to understand that as there is a real presence of Adam in all his children, so there is a real Presence of Christ in all His members." And believing this, as the Church always has believed it; believing, as St. Leo † says, that "by the grace of Christ we are transformed into the very flesh of Him who by His Incarnation took ours;" believing, with Bishop Andrews,‡ that "Christ has gone to the root and repaired our nature from the very foundation, so that what had been there defiled and decayed by the first Adam might be cleansed and set right again;" believing, with the learned Dean Jackson, that "Christ's humanity is the organ or conduit by which we are united and rec-

---

* Malcolm MacColl: "Christianity in Relation to Science," p. 244.

† St. Leo, quoted by Wilberforce on "The Incarnation," p. 206.

‡ Bishop Andrews, Sermon ix., on "The Nativity."

onciled unto the Divine Nature;" believing this old Gospel, the Church is able to go into the dark places of the earth with confidence; she has a remedy for the moral wrecks of humanity.*

She tells society that she need not exterminate by poison or the rifle the poor wretched Margarets of modern life; she need not drown or strangle their babes. For she has a power that will match these unseen powers of hell. She will cleanse one nature by another. The false shall be purged by the true.

We cannot, indeed, give the poor girl that crouches along the streets in her first shame the stainless nature of a mother whose family has not for generations known impurity; we cannot give the low, cunning Arab the inheritance of a Gordon or a Washington: but, though the nature of the great and pure on earth be closed to them, the nature of the God-Man is open. Though they cannot be children of women like Sister Dora or Catharine of Siena, they can be the children of Christ; though they cannot receive a mere earthly nature that has been for years and years self disciplined, honest and faithful, they can receive a divine nature that has known no weakness, no sin—a nature human in its sympathies, but divine in its strength.

We have seen our need; we have seen the

---

* Jackson's Comm. on the Creed, xi. 3-12.

gracious provision Christ has made for us—how it answers to our necessities; we must now show by what system it is conveyed to us. And to this there are in the main three different answers:

(1) That by the Incarnation this provision is in every man, for Christ is the Head of every man.

(2) That it is external to us, but we receive it by direct spiritual contact of faith without the interposition of any means.

(3) That it is given through divinely authorized means and received by faith.

The first of these requires our earnest attention, because that or a doctrine not very far removed from it is for reasons which I need not now give, becoming widely popular in our sadly divided Christendom.

It owes whatever strength it has to the apparent narrowness which seems, though it really does not, to characterize the second and third. It is a Gospel, so it is claimed, which appeals to every man. "Tell men they are children of God; that Christ indwells them and they indwell Christ; open their eyes to what they have, not to what they are without; proclaim them by nature children of grace, and tell them they have but to make an effort to reach the glorious possibilities of their future;" this is the modern Gospel. In this system sacraments are helps indeed, but rather as pictures, as symbolizing what has already taken place. They may even, so it is said, be described in the words of the Catechism as " means of grace," inasmuch as they serve to help men to realize what they would otherwise forget, just as the wedding-ring reminds the married of their privileges and responsibilities.

This theory, which has such a fascination about it, inasmuch as it brings the mighty workings of God more nearly within our comprehension, and flatters our poor, weak human nature, is open to grave and serious objection.

(1) It fails to take account of the many passages in which our Lord takes pains to emphasize the fact that in spite of the Incarnation man's natural condition is so far a wreck that nothing but the external intervention of God can restore it; that though the Incarnation was indeed the taking of the manhood into God, did indeed confer marvellous benefits on the whole race, yet each individual must be personally incorporated into Christ. Instead of looking upon men as naturally inside the Kingdom, He told them they must be born again in order to enter it; instead of telling men they were in Him and He in them, He bids them come to Him that they may have life; instead of looking upon the individuals composing the race as already His members, He bids His disciples by baptizing them to make them His members.

(2) It ignores the great truth of mediation which underlies all our Lord's teaching—that truth which He expressed when He said: "No man cometh unto the Father but by Me. I am the Door. He that entereth not by the Door, but climbeth up some other way, is a thief and a robber."* According to its conception, man is born in possession of divine life, though he may know it not. He consequently needs nothing but the inspiring example of the Saviour to reach his ideal; hence the all-important place that preaching occupies in this system. Our Lord's mediation is thus reduced to the inspiration of a prophet. Our Lord is by the side of the soul urging, exhorting, directing as one man may do to another, but is in no proper sense a mediator, a channel through which we may reach God.

(3) By virtually assuming that the sacraments are only forms of ritual, it at once encounters serious difficulties.

We are to suppose that our Lord on the night in which He was betrayed—that night when, as the torn veil plainly showed, shadows were to give place to substances—was replacing one pattern by another, was removing the time-honored and exceedingly suggestive ritual of the Passover by the comparatively dumb ritual of Bread and Wine.

---

* John xiv. 6; x., 9, 1.

SACRAMENTAL SYSTEM. 179

We are to suppose that on almost the last occasion when He appeared on earth, He is sending His little force of eleven men to conquer the world with a bare ceremony and a body of teaching.

We are to suppose that this empty ritual of Baptism, which has no more significance than a ring, could, within a very few years of our Lord's life, grow to such importance that on one occasion the journey of a high official of the court of Ethiopia must be stayed to perform it; that on another its urgency is considered of such important concern that it is performed in the middle of the night in the prison at Philippi, when the candidates for it have been rudely shaken by the excitement of a terrible earthquake; that on yet another it not only seals the reality of St. Paul's conversion, but itself is declared to be the means whereby His sins are to be washed away.

We are further to suppose, with regard to the other rite, that of the Lord's Supper, that our Lord has such concern about the right performance of what is only a religious ceremony, that He not only makes it a matter of special revelation to the mind of St. Paul, but strikes the Corinthians who profaned it with sickness—nay, even with death.

We are to suppose that within thirty years the Church's appreciation of these forms has become so extravagant that her writers—especially the very Apostle who is so fierce in his denunciation of every observance that takes the place of Christ—invest them with a majestic solemnity—St. Paul speaking of Baptism * as the work of the Holy Ghost, and of the Lord's Supper † as being "the sharing of the Body and Blood of Christ."

We are to suppose that the whole Church from the outset has surrounded simple rites with awe-inspiring language. St. Ignatius, ‡ an apostolic disciple, speaks of Baptism as the Christian's spiritual armor—of the Holy Eucharist as "the Bread of God." The Epistle of Barnabas,§ written within at least fifty years of St. John's death, boldly declares that we go down into the water full of sins and pollutions, but come up again bringing forth fruit. Justin Martyr, writing a little later, asserts that we do not receive in the Eucharist common bread and common drink, but the flesh and blood of the Incarnate Lord. Tertullian ‖ dares to call Holy Baptism "the blessed sacrament of water." We are to suppose that this lofty language investing these simple rites with mystery was created at a time when their celebration in bare rooms, caves, and holes of the earth was necessarily of the severest and most simple character. A splendid ritual might

---

* 1 Cor. xii. 13. † 1 Cor. x. 16. ‡ Ad. Polyc. vii.
§ C. 12. ‖ Apol. i. 93; De Baptismo, c. 1.

perhaps blind the eyes of the weak and force poetry and metaphorical language from the heart of emotional Easterns, but not these quiet, secret, severely simple Eucharists of the first Christians.

But again, their conduct is as strange as their words.

We are to suppose that such a strange devotion for ritual has sprung up that even prudent men and gentle women will of their own mind break the laws of the empire, brave the fierce emperor's wrath, excite the cupidity of the spy, court horrible deaths rather than forego the privilege of their daily or weekly Eucharist.

Nay, my brethren, we are asked too much. The language and practice of Apostles and Saints refuses to bend to this interpretation; and why should it? Why must we believe that the mind of an age which seems singularly wanting in that heroic self sacrifice which marked those first days is likely to discern the voice of the Lord more clearly than that of Sub-Apostolic times?

Why must we believe that an age when the Word of the living Lord is treated by large numbers of Christians with but scant reverence is likely to possess that devout insight which alone can penetrate the mysteries of the Church? Nay, we see no reason for reversing the estimate of the first two centuries by that of the nineteenth.

II. Let us now look at the second answer that is made. Grace is external to us, but we receive it immediately without the interposition of means.

This, if measured by the standard of the Word of God is much more complete than the first. It acknowledges the grace of our Lord Jesus Christ as a power external to the soul; it confesses that only through that grace can we hope to see the Father. Its main objection to the sacramental system is that grace is conferred through means. "The union and contact between Christ and His people," it asserts, "is immediate, spiritual; nothing is to be between"—not the most venerable and Apostolic organization, not the most precious of Christ-given ordinances."*

Now if this were seriously maintained, spiritual growth would be impossible.

If nothing is to be between the soul and Christ, then a mother's instruction, the words of the Scriptures, the voice of the preacher, must be set aside. A logical carrying out of the principle is impossible. But not only is the principle impracticable, but its most serious objection lies here: that it gives no opportunity to man for the exercise of his free-will; there is never any definite time when he is to exercise his choice. If nothing is to be between God and the soul, then how

---

* "Thoughts on Christian Sanctity," H. C. G. Moule, p. 109.

can man know when any appeal is made to him? This leads of necessity to the idea that we are verily as clay in the hands of the potter not in the sense of St. Paul, but in the sense of Calvin. Again, there is no external sign of God's election left to the individual, and place is made for those terrible subjective struggles through which some have lost their reason. The Church's teaching with regard to Infant Baptism, on the contrary, secures the impartiality of God's love, widens the number of the elect, stirs men to make the most of their possession, excites the imagination, influences the will. We know when God touched us—we are not left a prey to the terrors or dreams of our emotions. Our Baptismal Register declares that Christ has claimed us for His own and lives within us. This second answer, taken logically, results in that Calvinism which many leading Presbyterians in this country are endeavoring to discard from their confession of faith.

III. We turn now to the third answer, that which the Church gives. I need not occupy your time with statements as to her belief. "I believe one Baptism for the remission of sins" is her charter. It has been variously expanded, but with one consistent principle throughout—viz., that grace is ordinarily conferred through the sacraments. The Anglican branch of the Catholic Church speaks clearly: Sacraments are "means of grace given unto us"—*efficacia signa gratiæ*—"signs of grace which effect something"—"through which God works invisibly in us, not only quickening but strengthening faith." "In such as worthily receive them they have a wholesome effect or operation."

We claim three grounds in justification of this judgment of the Catholic Church:—(1) It is reasonable; (2) It is more in harmony with the spirit and letter of Christianity; and (3) It is deeply religious.

(1) It is reasonable. If there is one fact more than another which modern thought is fond of asserting it is the solidarity of the race.

That phrase means briefly that no man liveth to himself and dieth to himself, but that the individual is placed in such a dependence upon the race that to live apart from it is to stagnate. Our natural life is sacramental from beginning to end. As our physical existence depends for its growth on the life which is given through animal or vegetable food, so our mental life upon the words or writings of others. We cannot live without the mediation of others. All the objections commonly brought against the sacramental system of spiritual power may be brought against the sacramental system of natural power. For example one objection is, "Means will surely be exalted into ends," and so great was this danger with the Israelites that they were given forty years in the terrible Wilderness to learn that man does not "live by bread alone." Men have abused the sacramental system of nature in precisely the direction it was feared they might, and yet God has not abandoned it. He is forever teaching us that there is no antithesis such as we suppose between the spiritual and natural. As man's physical and mental natures are being built up through outward means, it is not unlikely, nay, it is probable, the same method will be adopted with our spiritual nature.

And as it is reasonable, so (2) it is in harmony with the spirit as well as the letter of God's revelation.

Adam and Eve are to grow to their full development by the Tree of Life; the Patriarchs find God's presence in particular places; the Tabernacle and Temple with their ceremonies, the Festivals with their services, alike emphasize the respect God has to outward means. Forms of color, waves of sound, actual material substances, are all used to convey certain blessings to man. And the sum of sacramental religion is reached in the Incarnation—when the Eternal Word takes not only the spirit and mind, but the human substance of the flesh of man, into God. That is the great sacrament. And as it presupposes a sacramental past, so it prophecies a sacramental future. Our Lord would seem to have taken pains to show us this. In His own healings of the bodies of men, which St. John tells us were signs of His spiritual healing, He constantly chooses outward means. Now it is water—now clay—now His garment—now His hand. And St. Luke suggests that the hand was His common method of healing. "When the sun was setting, all they that had any sick with divers diseases brought them unto Him, and He laid His hands on every one of them." In only five out of twenty-two recorded cases does He dispense with material means. It is only in accord, then, with His usual method of working when He "sanctifies water to the mystical washing away of sin," and consecrates bread and wine to be the means whereby we receive His Body and His Blood.

As it is reasonable, as it is in harmony with the known methods of our Lord's working, so (3) it is deeply religious.

May I very briefly suggest three points which will illustrate this:

(1) It appeals to the highest faith.

"The Lord's Supper," writes the Wesleyan scholar Dr. Beet,* "affords the severest test of our faith that Christ is actually and supernaturally

---
* Symposium on the Lord's Supper.

present and active among His people. It requires little or no faith in God to believe that a preached word may do good, for the connection between the means and the end is evident. But to expect spiritual grace from material bread and wine implies an acknowledgment of utter inability to obtain by our own intelligence the nourishment we require and a reliance upon the superhuman presence and power, and the faithfulness of Him who fed the five thousand, made water into wine and has promised to supply all His people's need by His own presence in their hearts to the end of time."

(2) It stimulates.

It not only calls for faith—arouses it—but helps it: we are constantly being stimulated to higher purposes by the sacraments. For they are, as Hooker * tells us, marks whereby we know when God doth impart the vital or saving grace of Christ unto all that are capable thereof. " Since God is invisible, therefore when it seemeth good in the eyes of His heavenly wisdom that men for some special intent and purpose should take notice of His glorious Presence, He giveth them some plain and sensible token whereby to know what they cannot see. Christ and His Holy Spirit, with all their blessed effects, though entering into the soul of man, we are not able to apprehend or express

---
* Hooker, v., lvii. 3.

how, notwithstanding give notice of the times when they use to make their access because it pleaseth Almighty God to communicate by sensible means those blessings which are incomprehensible."

(3) It teaches charity as none other can.

There is indeed something touching in the drawing out of men's sympathies one toward another in the solemn meeting together and remembering the Lord in the way He has appointed; but it amounts to little more than a sentiment, an emotion. But the realization that the man who kneels beside me is receiving the nature of Christ not only sheds a glow about his life, but makes one feel that our union is not based on the recollection of a common mercy, unspeakable as it is, but on the common possession of a divine life.

(4) Lastly, this system preaches hope as none other can.

Since through the sacraments we are partakers of the Divine nature, since by them Christ indwells us and we Him, then there is no height to which we may not climb, no path of holiness too difficult. We at once dismiss the mere worldly standard of morality as entirely too low for such a divine power and strength as that with which we are gifted. We welcome every passage of that high standard of the Sermon on the Mount, not only as possibilities for the child of the saint, but for the child of the unclean; not only for the child of the Fifth Avenue, but for the child of the Bowery.

And we are confident that this world of ours, scarred with its battlefields, darkened with its ignorance and vice, defiled with the unceasing impurities of men, is yet crowned with a halo of light, bathed in an atmosphere of holiness, for upon it stands the form of the Son of Man, and radiating from Him these streams of never-ceasing grace.

It seems scarcely necessary to say that the Church Club is not responsible for any individual opinions on points, not ruled by the Church, which, the learned theologians who have been good enough to lecture under its auspices, may have expressed.

www.ingramcontent.com/pod-product-compliance
Lightning Source LLC
Chambersburg PA
CBHW020908230426
43666CB00008B/1354